SKILLS & RULES
VOLLEYBALL

Vivek Solanki

KHEL SAHITYA KENDRA
/26, Ansari Road, Daryaganj,
New Delhi-110002

Published by:
KHEL SAHITYA KENDRA
7/26, Ansari Road, Darya Ganj, New Delhi-110002
Ph.: (O) 011-65190343, 43551324, 42564726
(M) 9811088729, (Fax) 011-42564726
(Res.) 47091605
E-mail: khelsahitya1@rediffmail.com
Web: www.khelsahitya.com, www.kskpublisher.com

ISBN 978-81-7524-577-8

PRINTED IN INDIA 2025

Printed by:
ASIAN OFFSET PRINTERS
Delhi

Laser Typesetting by:
JAIN MEDIA GRAPHICS
Delhi

Contents

1

INTRODUCTION AND HISTORY OF VOLLEYBALL

Volleyball is an Olympic team sport in which two teams of 6 players are separated by a net. Each team tries to score points by grounding a ball on the other team's court under organized rules. This article focuses on competitive indoor volleyball; numerous other variations of volleyball have developed, most notably the Olympic spin-off sport beach volleyball.

The complete rules are extensive. But simply, play proceeds as follows: A player on one of the teams begins a rally by serving the ball (tossing or releasing it and

then hitting it with a hand or arm), from behind the back boundary line of the court, over the net, and into the receiving team's court. The receiving team must not let the ball be grounded within their court. They may touch the ball as many as three times. Typically, the first two touches to set up for an attack, an attempt to direct the ball back over the net in such a way that the serving team is unable to prevent it from being grounded in their court.

The rally continues, with each team allowed as many as three consecutive touches, until either (1): a team makes a kill, grounding the ball on the opponent's court and winning the rally; or (2): a team commits a fault and loses the rally. The team that wins the rally is awarded a point, and serves the ball to start the next rally. A few of the most common faults include:

- causing the ball to touch the ground outside the opponents' court or without first passing over the net;
- catching and throwing the ball;
- double hit: two consecutive contacts with the ball made by the same player;
- four consecutive contacts with the ball made by the same team.

The ball is usually played with the hands or arms, but players can legally strike or push (short contact) the ball with any part of the body.

A number of consistent techniques have evolved in volleyball, including spiking and blocking (because these plays are made above the top of the net the vertical jump is an athletic skill emphasized in the sport) as well as passing, setting, and specialized player positions and offensive and defensive structures.

ORIGIN OF VOLLEYBALL

On February 9, 1895, in Holyoke, Massachusetts (USA), William G Morgan, a YMCA physical education director, created a new game called Mintonette as a pastime to be played preferably indoors and by any number of players. The game took some of its characteristics from tennis and handball. Another indoor sport, basketball, was catching on in the area, having been invented just ten miles (sixteen kilometers) away in the city of Springfield, Massachusetts, only four years before. Mintonette was designed to be an indoor sport less rough than basketball for older members of the YMCA, while still requiring a bit of athletic effort.

The first rules, written down by William G Morgan, called for a net 6 ft 6 in (1.98 m) high, a 25×50 ft (7.6×15.2 m) court, and any number of players. A match was composed of nine innings with three serves for each team in each inning, and no limit to the number of ball contacts for each team before sending the ball to the opponents' court. In case of a serving error, a second try was allowed. Hitting the ball into the net was considered a foul (with loss of the point or a side-out)—except in the case of the first-try serve.

After an observer, Alfred Halstead, noticed the volleying nature of the game at its first exhibition match in 1896, played at the International YMCA Training School (now called Springfield College), the game quickly became known as volleyball (it was originally spelled as two words: "volley ball"). Volleyball rules were slightly modified by the International YMCA Training School and the game spread around the country to various YMCAs.

REFINEMENTS AND LATER DEVELOPMENTS

The first official ball used in volleyball is disputed; some sources say that Spalding created the first official ball in 1896, while others claim it was created in 1900. The rules have evolved over time; In Philippines by 1916, the skill and power of the set and spike had been introduced, and four years later a "three hits" rule and a rule against hitting from the back row were established. In 1917, the game was changed from 21 to 15 points. In 1919, about 16,000 volleyballs were distributed by the American Expeditionary Forces to their troops and allies, which sparked the growth of volleyball in new countries.

The first country outside the United States to adopt volleyball was Canada in 1900. An international federation, the Fédération Internationale de Volleyball (FIVB), was founded in 1947, and the first World Championships were held in 1949 for men and 1952 for women. The sport is now popular in Brazil, in Europe (where especially Italy, the Netherlands, and countries from Eastern Europe have been major forces since the late 1980s), in Russia, and in other countries including China and the rest of Asia, as well in as the United States.

Beach volleyball, a variation of the game played on sand and with only two players per team, became a FIVB-endorsed variation in 1987 and was added to the Olympic program at the 1996 Summer Olympics. Volleyball is also a sport at the Paralympics managed by the World Organisation Volleyball for Disabled.

VOLLEYBALL IN THE OLYMPICS

The history of Olympic volleyball traces back to the 1924 Summer Olympics in Paris, where volleyball was played as part of an American sports demonstration event. After the foundation of FIVB and some continental confederations, it began to be considered for official inclusion. In 1957, a special tournament was held at the 53rd IOC session in Sofia, Bulgaria to support such request. The competition was a success, and the sport was officially included in the program for the 1964 Summer Olympics.

The Olympic volleyball tournament was originally a simple competition, whose format paralleled the one still employed in the World Cup: all teams played against each other team and then were ranked by wins, set average, and point average. One disadvantage of this

round-robin system is that medal winners could be determined before the end of the games, making the audience lose interest in the outcome of the remaining matches. To cope with this situation, the competition was split into two phases with the addition of a "final round" elimination tournament consisting of quarterfinals, semifinals, and finals matches in 1972. The number of teams involved in the Olympic tournament has grown steadily since 1964. Since 1996, both men's and women's events count twelve participant nations. Each of the five continental volleyball confederations has at least one affiliated national federation involved in the Olympic Games.

The U.S.S.R. won men's gold in both 1964 and 1968. After taking bronze in 1964 and silver in 1968, Japan finally won the gold for men's volleyball in 1972. Women's gold went to Japan in 1964 and again in 1976. That year, the introduction of a new offensive skill, the backrow attack, allowed Poland to win the men's competition over the Soviets in a very tight five-set match. Since the strongest teams in men's volleyball at the time belonged to the Eastern Bloc, the American-led boycott of the 1980 Summer Olympics did not have as great an effect on these events as it had on the women's. The U.S.S.R. collected their third Olympic Gold Medal in men's volleyball with a 3-1 victory over Bulgaria (the Soviet women won that year as well, their third gold as well). With the U.S.S.R. boycotting the 1984 Olympic Games in Los Angeles, the U.S. was able to sweep Brazil in the finals to win the men's gold medal. Italy won its first medal (bronze in the men's competition) in 1984, foreshadowing a rise in prominence for their volleyball teams.

At the 1988 Games, Karch Kiraly and Steve Timmons led the U.S. men's team to a second straight gold medal. In 1992, underrated Brazil upset favourites C.I.S., Netherlands, and Italy in the men's competition for the country's first Olympic gold medal. Runner-up Netherlands, men's silver medalist in 1992, came back under team leaders Ron Zwerver and Olof van der Meulen in the 1996 Games for a five-set win over Italy. A men's bronze medalist in 1996, Serbia and Montenegro (playing in 1996 and 2000 as the Federal Republic of Yugoslavia) beat Russia in the gold medal match in 2000, winning their first gold medal ever. In 2004, Brazil won its second men's volleyball gold medal beating Italy in the finals. In the 2008 Games, the USA beat Brazil in the men's volleyball final.

Volleyball is played in more than sixty countries and by more than sixty million people. In countries in Eastern Europe, Asia and South America top games draw crowds the size of which rival those at soccer matches. At world championship matches it's not unusual to see ticket touts doing business on a scale that we in England would see only at the F.A. Cup Final. As a recreational team sport volleyball ranks as about the third most popular in the world and is considered as a top level competitive sport in more than twenty countries.

The game of volleyball was invented in 1895 by William Morgan, who worked for the Y.M.C.A. in Holyoak, Massachusetts. He was concerned with providing exercise for large groups of business men, and his earliest from of the game was designed to provide mild exercise for people of this kind. This original game was very simple— any number of players batted a basketball bladder backwards and forwards over a tennis net which was fixed at a height of six feet.

Since then the game has developed and spread world wide. It's early progress outside America is generally accepted to have followed the armed forces and the spread of the Y.M.C.A. movement. It's fantastic increase in popularity can be explained by a host of reasons: it is basically a very simple game. It can be played indoors and outdoors, and is therefore suitable for varying seasons and any climate. The playing area required takes up comparatively little space so that play can take place in a gym, a sports hall, the park, the beach and even some more unlikely places like hangar decks of aircraft carriers, and it can be played by players of both sexes and over a considerable age range. The equipment required is simple and still relatively inexpensive. Play can be of tremendously varying standards, formal purely recreative level on the beach and in the park, through all levels of clubs and school competitions, right up to the supremely demanding and fiercely competitive play at international level.

The first attempts to organise the game internationally were made by representatives of twenty-two interested countries at the Berlin Olympics in 1936. Ten years later the Federation International de Volleyball was set up, with its headquarters in Paris, to administer and control volleyball throughout the world, The first world championships were organised in Prague in 1949. There are also various zonal championships, such as the European Championships. In 1964 volleyball became an Olympic sport for the first time when the Olympic Games were held in Tokyo.

The modern game is dominated at international level by national teams from japan and Eastern Europe. The society in which their players live make it possible for them to train and prepare for many hours every week, and the money available there from the paying public and from the governments make sure that training is not at the players expense. The sports schools and other facilities for coaches and trainers ensure that the technical expertise necessary to train players, is also available. The money and status available to coaches makes sure that there is no shortage of them. It seems unlikely that similar opportunities will be available in most of the western world. Neither does the culture encourage western players to train so hard and for so long. Therefore the Japanese and East European dominance is likely to continue.

The way in which the game is played now is a far cry from that designed by William Morgam. Decades of competition have produced increasingly well performed skills and a steady development of new tactics as coaches strive for ever higher standards of play. The rules of the game have been reviewed at regular intervals, with changes made when necessary to try to keep attack and defence well balanced, to produce long, closely fought rallies in order to maintain the game as an exciting spectator sport.

The basic pattern of the modern game of volleyball is as follows: the match is played between tow teams of up to twelve players, only six from each team are on court at one time. The game is played on a court eighteen meters long and nine metres wide. A net divides the court into two and separates the two teams. This net is fixed at a height of 2m.43cm. for men and at 2m.21cm. for women and youths.

Play is started by one player hitting the ball over the net from within the service area behind his own base line. Once the ball passes over the net receiving team may hit the ball three times before it must go back over the net. The ball is normally played on the hands or arms but the rules do allow contact with any part of the player's body above the waist. No player may touch the ball twice in succession unless his first touch was while blocking. The receiving team may play the ball back over the net on the first, second or third touch, but at competitive level it is necessary to use all three touches to build up a strong attack. Any variations on this patterns are used for their surprise value. The object of the game is to ground the ball on the floor within the opponents' half of the court, or to play the ball over in such a way as to pressure them so much that they play the ball illegally or are unable to return the ball over the net and into court.

The first touch is usually used to play the ball up close to the net, the second touch is the set. This allows the attack to be completed by a player running in and jumping up to smash the ball downwards over the net into the opponents' court. To defend against this, one, two or three of the opposing team jump together to intercept the smashed ball and block its path with their hands, trying to force the ball back down into the attackers' court. If the blockers do not succeed in stopping the smash the remaining defending players attempt to control the ball before it hits the floor so that their team can build up an attack of their own.

If the serving team win a really they score a point. If the receiving side win the rally they are awarded a "side-out" and win the right to serve next. When a team win the right to serve they rotate one place round so that all players have to serve and play in both front and back lines. The team researching fifteen points first wins the set, unless the score was fourteen each, when play must continue until one team has a lead of two points. A game can be either to the best of three or five sets.

The coach can influence the play of his team during a game in three ways: he can take two time-outs every set, each a thirty-second break in play, during which he can talk to his team. He can make six substitutions during each set, and between sets he can again talk to his team and make changes to it for the next set. Apart from this, no coaching is allowed from the side of the court.

The game is controlled by two referees. The first is seated level with the net and high enough to see along it. He has overall charge of the game. He is assisted by a second referee on the floor on the opposite side of the court. There are also either two or four lines-men, depending on the standard of the game, to assist in deciding whether a ball lands in or out of the area of the court. A scorer completes the match officials.

POPULARITY

Volleyball began to become popular. The game was introduced to the Philippines in 1910, to Japan in 1913, to Poland in 1915, to Uruguay in 1916, to Brazil and Latvia in 1919, and to Syria in 1922. After World War I, it was introduced throughout Europe.

While the YMCA kept volleyball as an indoor game, the Playground of America started to teach it as an outdoor game after their convention in 1907.

In the early 1920s, the University of Illinois began to teach volleyball as a physical education activity. The university also began an intramural program featuring volleyball competition.

The first college team was started in Oregon in 1928. The University of Washington followed with a team in 1934. These teams played in recreational leagues. The first university volleyball league began in 1941 with 12 teams, among them teams from Columbia, Temple, and the University of Pennsylvania.

By the late 1940s many colleges fielded club teams, and by 1952 the NCAA was willing to sponsor national championships if eight schools were ready to field varsity teams. While many colleges fielded club teams, only six were ready with varsity teams at that time.

The United States Volleyball Association was formed in 1928, and by 1937 it controlled the game in the United States. In 1947, the International Volleyball Federation was formed to regulate the game throughout the world. Fifteen nations sent representatives. By 1953 the first World Championships were held, in 1955 volleyball was played in the first Pan American Games, and in 1964 it became an Olympic sport.

The popularity of the game today is evidenced by the rapid increase in players. A recent poll showed that 800 million people in the world now play volleyball at atleast once a week. Of the 50 sports listed in the survey, volleyball was the twelfth most popular sport. Further, the poll showed that in the last 25 years the sport had increased in popularity by 500 percent and that it is growing even more rapidly today, with 46 million

Americans now playing the game. The increasing popularity over the years can be credited to the YMCA and physical education programs in high schools and colleges. In fact, more people now participate in volleyball than in tennis, soccer, skiing, golf, or baseball.

While the game is most popular among the 25 to 35 age group. It is quickly attracting a following among the young. During the last five years youth volleyball has doubled in popularity and is the fastest-growing sport among young Americans. Interscholastic volleyball is the third most popular sport for girls. And boys teams are rapidly being implemented across the country. In one recent year more than 50 boys' teams were instituted in New York City alone!

As spectator sports, the international game and the beach game continue to attract fans both at the game and on television. As the spectators' knowledge of the game increases, the demand increases for more games. And the demands of television have even influenced rule changes designed to fit the volleyball game into a specific time dimension.

According to J.D. Giles, the ideal of the human race is for individuals to develop a strong, positive character. This often proves difficult, as the development of character may result in either positive or negative traits. The statement by Hill that Games are valuable only as they leave their mark upon the character of the individuals participating may be considered in relation to volleyball.

The fellowship accompanying the game can lead to fun and socially rewarding experiences. Individuals may play for fun and relaxation or for intensely competitive championships. In both situations, the players often fraternize while participating and develop deep and lasting friendships. Courtesy, cooperation, loyalty and agreeableness are positive values in character development. Without these, a volleyball player or team does not function efficiently.

A recreational or competitive game presents many playing situations that test these qualities. A negative attitude can cause problems between teammates, between opponents, or with the officials. Team play and individual improvement are dependent upon these values' being positive rather than negative. Volleyball provides an opportunity to strengthen one's moral judgement, honesty, fairmindedness, and sportsmanship have been three of the strongest values of the sport from its very beginning. The spirit and tradition of volleyball has been to call your own fouls when they were undetected by officials.

Other values associated with volleyball are precision, determination, persistence, and alertness. Volleyball, when played skilfully and competitively, requires individual and team precision. A player must attempt to master the fundamentals in every skill area. The speed of the game requires precise timing and alertness for ultimate ball control. Every player has specific responsibilities, which change rapidly. Any breakdown in precise coverage weakens the team, as do skill deficiencies. Developing into an all-round player takes both determination and persistence. The carry over value of the sport is a great contribution to society. It is one of the few team sports in which an individual can actively participate, recreationally or competitively for a lifetime.

In 1895 William G. Morgan, an instructor at the Young Men's Christian Association (YMCA) in Holyoke, Mass, decided to blend elements of basketball, baseball, tennis, and handball to create a game for his classes of businessmen which would demand less physical contact than basketball. He created the game of Volleyball (at that time called mintonette). Morgan borrowed the net from tennis, and raised it 6 feet 6 inches above the floor, just above the average man's head. Morgan originally called his new game of Volleyball, Mintonette. The name Volleyball came about after a demonstration game of the sport, when a spectator commented that the game involved much "volleying" and game was renamed Volleyball.

William Morgan was born in the state of New York and studied at Springfield College, Massachusetts. Ironically at Springfield, Morgan met James Naismith who invented basketball in 1891. Morgan was motivated by Naismith's game of basketball designed for younger students to invent a game suitable for the older members of the YMCA. William Morgan's basis for the new game of Volleyball was the then popular and similar German game of Faustball and a few other sports including: tennis (the net), basketball, baseball and handball.

The Morgan Trophy Award is presented annually to the most outstanding male and female collegiate volleyball player in the United States. Established by the William G. Morgan Foundation in 1995 during the centennial year of volleyball, the trophy is named in honor of William Morgan.

During a demonstration game, someone remarked to Morgan that the players seemed to be volleying the ball back and forth over the net, and perhaps "volleyball" would be a more descriptive name for the sport.

The first game of volleyball was played on July 7, 1896 at Springfield College

A special ball was designed for the sport in 1990

In 1916, in the Philippines, an offensive style of passing the ball in a high trajectory to be struck by another player (the set and spike) were introduced. The Filipinos developed the "bomba" or kill, and called the hitter a "bomberino".

In 1920, three hits per side and back row attack rules were instituted.

In 1934, the approval and recognition of national volleyball referees.

In 1964, Volleyball was introduced to the Olympic Games in Tokyo.

In 1995, the sport of Volleyball was 100 years old!

The sport originated in the United States, and is now just achieving the type of popularity in the U.S. that it has received on a global basis, where it ranks behind only soccer among participation sports.

Today there are more than 46 million Americans who play volleyball. There are 800 million players worldwide who play Volleyball at least once a week.

In 2009, the sport of Volleyball is 114 years old!

The sport originated in the United States, and is now just achieving the type of popularity in the U.S. that it has received on a global basis, where it ranks behind only soccer among participation sports.

Today there are more than 46 million Americans who

play volleyball. There are 800 million players worldwide who play volleyball at least once a week.

During a demonstration game, someone remarked to Morgan that the players seemed to be volleying the ball back and forth over the net, and perhaps "volleyball" would be a more descriptive name for the sport. On July 7, 1896 at Springfield College the first game of "volleyball" was played.

1895: William G. Morgan (1870-1942) created the game of volleyball.

1900: a special ball was designed for the sport.

1916: in the Philippines, an offensive style of passing the ball in a high trajectory to be struck by another player (the set and spike) were introduced.

1917: the game was changed from 21 to 15 points.

1920s: there are unconfirmed whispers of men's teams playing on the beach in Hawaii, but most accounts place the sport's origin in Santa Monica, California where the first Volleyball courts are put up on the beach at the Playground. Families play 6 vs. 6..

1920: three hits per side and back row attack rules were instituted.

1922: the first YMCA national championships were held in Brooklyn, NY. 27 teams from 11 states were represented.

1928: it became clear that tournaments and rules were needed, the United States Volleyball Association (USVBA, now USA Volleyball) was formed. The first U.S. Open was staged, as the field was open to non-YMCA squads.

1930s: the first two-man beach volleyball game is played in Santa Monica, California..

1934: the approval and recognition of national volleyball referees.

1937: at the AAU convention in Boston, action was taken to recognize the U.S. Volleyball Association as the official National Governing Body (NGB) in the U.S.

1947: the Federation Internationale De Volley-Ball (FIVB) was founded.

1948: the first two-man beach tournament was held.

1949: the initial World Championships were held in Prague, Czechoslovakia.

1964: Volleyball was introduced to the Olympic Games in Tokyo.

1965: the California Beach Volleyball Association (CBVA) was formed.

1974: the World Championships in Mexico were telecast in Japan.

1975: the U.S. National Women's team began a year-round training regime in Pasadena, Texas (moved to Colorado Springs in 1979, Coto de Caza and Fountain Valley, CA in 1980, and San Diego, CA in 1985).

1977: the U.S. National Men's team began a year-round training regime in Dayton, Ohio (moved to San Diego, CA in 1981).

1983: the Association of Volleyball Professionals (AVP) was formed.

1984: the U.S. won their first medals at the Olympics in Los Angeles. The Men won the Gold, and the Women the Silver.

1986: the Women's Professional Volleyball Association (WPVA) was formed.

1988: the U.S. Men repeated the Gold in the Olympics in Korea.

1989: the FIVB Sports Aid Program was created.

1990: the World League was created.

1995: the sport of Volleyball was 100 years old! This Website - Volleyball.Com goes live!

1996: 2-person beach volleyball debuted as an Olympic Sport.

1997: Dain Blanton (with Canyon Ceman) becomes the first African-American professional beach volleyball player to win a tournament on the Miller Lite/AVP Tour.

1998: For the first time in the FIVB World Tour, men and women players are rewarded at the same level with $170,000 in total prize money per Open event.

1999: For the first time beach volleyball was included in the Pan American Games which were held in Canada.

2000: Olympic Beach Volleyball Men's Gold medallists: Eric Fomoimoana & Dain Blanton (USA). The women's Beach Volleyball America (BVA) announces their inaugural season of play.

2001: Christopher "Sinjin" Smith plays the final match of his impressive career, a 21-19 and 24-22 loss with George Roumain to Dax Holdren and Todd Rogers in the 4th round of the contender's bracket at the AVP Manhattan Beach Open. Sinjin retires as the leader in tournaments played with 416, 2nd in all-time victories with 139, and 4th in all-time winnings with over US$1.6 million earned.

2002: Beach volleyball court dimensions reduced to 8m × 8m per side.

2003: Karch Kiraly becomes the first player to earn US$3M in prize money and oldest player to win an AVP tournament at age 42 years, 9 months and 14 days. (You're never too old for volleyball!)

2004: Kerri Walsh and Misty May Win the Women's Olympic Beach Volleyball Title

2005: Olympic gold medalists Kerri Walsh and Misty May-Treanor win their second Association of Volleyball Professionals (AVP) Open women's title and the 2005 overall women's championship.

2006: Elaine Youngs' second place finish (with Rachel Wacholder) in Seaside Heights pushes her career earnings past $1 million. She becomes the third American woman to achieve that mark.

2006: In Seaside Heights, both Casey Jennings (with Matt Fuerbringer) and Kerri Walsh (with Misty May-Treanor) won titles, becoming just the second husband-wife duo to win pro beach events on the same weekend. They join Mike and Patty Dodd, who accomplished the feat four times in 1989, but each time in different locations.

2006: Kerri Walsh and Misty May-Treanor win in Chicago as Walsh joins the millionaire club. She is the 18th person worldwide to win over $1 million in her career, and did so in fewer events (90th tournament) as well as being one of just four to reach the mark before

South America. The set and spike was first executed in the Philippines. This offensive system altered how the game was played. For the first time the ball was set in a high trajectory and then spiked by a teammate. The Filipinos created the kill, known in United States as bomba. The bomba was named after the attacker called the bomberino.

Rules and tournaments came about as a result of the formation of the United States Volleyball Association USVBA. The first U.S. Open was staged, as the field was open to non-YMCA squads. The United States Volleyball Association (USVBA) was formed in 1928 and recognized as the rules-making, governing body in the United States.

Since 1928, the USVBA, now known as USA Volleyball (USAV), has put on national men's and senior men's (age 35 and older) volleyball championships every year except during 1944 and 1945.

Women's USVBA divisions started in 1949 and have been growing ever since.

In the late 1940s, some European national federations began discussing the need for creating an international governing body for the sport of volleyball.

The FIVB was founded in Paris, France in 1947. Initial discussions eventually lead to the installation of a Constitutive Congress in 1947. Fourteen national federations representing five different continents attended meetings where the organization was officially formed.

One of the main goals of the 1947 Congress was achieved two years later with the establishment of the

first international major volleyball event, the World Championship.

In 1952, a women played in FIVB tournaments for the first time in volleyball history.

For the first time in the history of volleyball, volleyball was played in the Pan American Games in 1955.

In 1957, volleyball was designated as an Olympic team sport by the International Olympic Committee (IOC).

In 1959, the International University Sports Federation (FISU) had volleyball be one of the eight competitions held in first University Games in Turin, Italy.

In 1960, seven midwestern institutions formed the Midwest Intercollegiate Volleyball Association (MIVA).

In the 1960's, new volleyball techniques were developed. Off-speed hits, open hand tips, forearm passing, blocking at the net, and defensive plays such as diving and sprawling become a big part of the game.

With the FIVB already having its own world championships, the FIVB directed its attention to the Olympic Games. Thanks to the Bulgarian Volleyball Federation, a tournament took place in Sofia in 1957 during the International Olympic Committee meetings. As a result of this event, volleyball became an Olympic Sport.

In 1964, volleyball was first played in the Olympics in Tokyo. Volleyball became a part of the Olympic Games, which allowed it to grow even more. Also, in the 1964 Olympics, the Japanese used a volleyball that consisted of a rubber casing with leather panels. A similar ball is used in modern volleyball competitions.

In 1969, a new international event, the World Cup was introduced. The World Cup would be turned into a qualifying event for the 1991 Olympic Games.

In 1974, Japan telecasted a major volleyball event in Mexico, the World Championships.

In 1983, the Association of Volleyball Professionals (AVP) was founded by Leonard Armato. The organization started its own beach volleyball tour in the United States in 1984.

By the late 1980's, the AVP tour was growing fast due to the promotion of the sport by the professional beach players Tim Hovland, Sinjin Smith, Randy Stoklos, and Mike Dodd.

In 1986, the Women's Professional Volleyball Association (WPVA) was formed to administer, govern, and protect the integrity of Women's Professional Beach Volleyball.

In 1987, the FIVB added a Beach Volleyball World Championship Series 1989 - The FIVB Sports Aid Program was created In 1990, a men's volleyball competition called the World League was created.

The World League is the longest and most flourishing of all the international events organized by the FIVB. The tournament is an annual event.

In 2006, prize money became a major deal with $20 million dollars being distributed amongst 16 participating teams from 5 continents. The World League is sometimes confused with the other international volleyball competitions – Volleyball World Cup and Volleyball World Championships.

In 1995, the sport of Volleyball turned 100 years old.

In 1996, for the first time in the history of volleyball, beach doubles volleyball is included in the Olympic Games.

Major events in the 90's took place including the establishment of annual competitions for men's and women's volleyball (the World League, in 1990, and the Grand Prix, in 1993), the indication of Beach volleyball as an Olympic event (1996). These events and many rule changes in the garne were made the purpose of enhancing the popularity and public visibility of the sport.

BEACH VOLLEYBALL HISTORY, THE BEGINNING...

In the 1920's, people start playing volleyball on the beaches of Hawaii. Also, many people say volleyball started in Santa Monica, California where they first started playing 6's on the beach.

In the 1930's, the first doubles beach volleyball game is played in Santa Monica, California. Also, in the 1930's beach volleyball appears for the first time in Europe.

In 1947, the first official two-man Beach Volleyball tournament is held at Will Rogers State Beach, California.

There wasn't any prize money. In 1948, the first prize money was given out at a tournament held in Los Angeles, California. The prize was a case of Pepsi.

In the 1950's, the first volleyball tour is organized by Parks & Rec. Five California beaches for the circuit are Santa Barbara, Will Rogers State Beach, Sorrento Beach, Laguna Beach, and San Diego. Also in the 1950's, the first volleyball tournament takes place in Brazil. The tournament is sponsored by a newspaper publishing.

The first Manhattan Beach Open in beach volleyball history takes place in 1960. In the 1960's, Open tournaments are held on thirteen beaches in California.

In 1970, the first Hermosa Beach tournament is played. Ron Von Hagen and Henry Bergman win the title.

In 1975, a tournament is held in San Diego, California. The tournament has 250 fans and $1,500 in total prize money. Dennis Hare and Fred Zeulich win the tournament.

In 1976, a beach volleyball tournament is held at Will Rogers State Beach. The tournament has a $5,000 first place prize and about 30,000 spectators. Also in 1976, Ron Von Hagen retires with 62 Open wins. Ron Von Hagen is now considered in beach volleyball history as the Babe Ruth of Beach Volleyball.

In 1978, Jose Cuervo Tequila becomes beach volleyballs first major sponsor. In 1979, Manhattan Beach has a King of the Beach Tournament. The prize money totals $11,000.

In 1980, the first beach volleyball sponsored tour had $52,000 in prize money. The tour had stops in San

Diego, Santa Barbara, Laguna Beach ($5,000), Manhattan Beach ($10,000), The King of the Beach ($12,000), and The World Championships ($15,000).

In 1981, another major sponsor joins beach volleyball, the Miller Brewing Company.

In 1982, the tour becomes national with $69,000 in total cash prizes awarded for six events.

In 1983, $137,000 in total cash prizes is awarded for 12 tournaments. The AVP is formed on July 21, to protect players' interests and to preserve the integrity of beach volleyball.

In 1984, the AVP Players go on strike. The AVP begins running its own tour. In 1985, the Bolle Sunglasses become a major AVP sponsor. The total tour prize money reaches $275,000.

In 1985, the AVP Tour includes stops in eight different states - California, Massachusetts, Arizona, Florida, Colorado, Illinois, New Jersey, and Hawaii. In

In 1986, AVP Pro Beach Volleyball receives cable television coverage and is shown for the first time in beach volleyball history on ABC's Wide World of Sports.

HISTORY OF BEACH VOLLEYBALL AND THE FÉDÉRATION INTERNATIONALE DE VOLLEYBALL (FIVB)

In 1986, the first international Beach Volleyball exhibition in Rio de Janeiro is held with 5,000 spectators. Also, at the Brazilian Volleyball Champions, beach volleyball players Jackie Silva, Isabel Salgado, Renan, Badá, William, Montanaro, Jackie Silva, Isabel Salgado, Vera Mossa, Regina Uchoa, along with the

American beach players Pat Powers and Sinjin Smith become leading figures in the international growth of Beach Volleyball. Also in 1986, the Australian Pro Beach Circuit starts.

In 1987, the first international FIVB sanctioned Beach Volleyball tournament is run in Rio de Janeiro, Brazil. The prize money is $22,000. Sinjin Smith and Randy Stoklos are the winners. In 1990, the first FIVB Beach Volleyball International Circuit has a total of $140,000 in prize money. The tournament is named the World Series and is made up of men's tournaments in Brazil, Italy, and Japan. Many fans are left standing out of the sold out stadium while Sinjin Smith and Randy Stoklos become the Men's World Champions.

In 1992, prize money reaches $950,000 for the Beach Volleyball World Series. The Series is made up of six events.

The first ever women's FIVB Beach Volleyball competition in the history of beach volleyball takes place in Almeria, Spain.

The first Women World Champions are Nancy Reno and Karolyn Kirby.

Sinjin Smith and Randy Stoklos become World Champions for the 5th time.

In 1993, for the first time in the history of beach volleyball, volleyball becomes an Olympic sport when the International Olympic Committee grants the sport medal status. Twenty-four men's teams and eighteen women's teams will compete for the first Beach Volleyball Olympic Gold Medal in the upcoming 1996 Atlanta Olympics.

Franco Neto and Roberto Lopes of Brazil are the first non-Americans to win the Men's World Champions. Karolyn Kirby and Liz Masakayan are the Women's World Champions.

In 1994, the FIVB Beach Volleyball World Series tops 1 million dollars in total prize money with twelve tournaments. In 1994, Beach Volleyball is included in the Goodwill Games held in St. Petersburg, Russia.

Brazil, United States, and Chile host Women's FIVB Beach Volleyball events.

The Men's World Champions are Jan Kvalheim and

Bjorn Maaseide (Norway) and the Women's World Champions are Mônica Rodrigues and Adriana Samuel (Brazil).

In 1995, the FIVB Beach Volleyball World Championship Series has 27 total tournaments for both the men and women providing $3.5 million in prize money.

Brazilian team Franco Neto and Roberto Lopes win the World Championships. Franco and Roberto set a record with seven tournament wins in the season. Jackie Silva and Sandra Pires are the Women's Champions.

In 1996, the FIVB Beach Volleyball World Championships Series holds 29 tournaments and prize money is up to $4.3 million.

The Brazilians Zé Marco and Emanuel Rego dominate the World Championships Jackie Silva and Sandra Pires win the Women's Championships. Rego sets the men's FIVB record for prize money in a season, $174,000.

In 1997, Brazilians Zé Marco and Emanuel Rego control the Tour Championships for the third straight year repeating as the Men's Champions. Adriana Behar and Shelda Bede win the Women's Championships.

In 1998, the first time in the history of beach volleyball FIVB World Tour, men and women players are rewarded the same total prize money, $170,000.

Teams receive information on how to qualify for the next Olympics. Twenty-four men's teams along with the same number of women's teams will compete in the 2000 Olympic Games in Sydney.

A huge television campaign gives great exposure to the World Tour.

Beach Volleyball is included as a major sport for the South East Asian Games, Central and Pan-American Games, and Universiade.

The FIVB introduces new opportunities to amateurs by providing Challenger, Satellite, and Amateur tournaments.

More than 120 National Federations now have regular Beach Volleyball events.

In 1999, the Men's and Women's World Championships are organized in Europe for the first time in the history of beach volleyball.

For the first time, Beach Volleyball is included in the Pan American Games.

Brazilians Jose Loiola and Emanuel Rego and

Adriana Behar and Shelda Bede dominate the World Championships again.

In 2000, Brazilians dominate the men's season with three teams combining to win nine of the thirteen events. The American women dominated the women's season with three teams finishing in the top four in rankings and combining to win seven of the thirteen events.

In 2004, Misty May and Kerri Walsh extend a winning streak to 14 tournament victories after beating Holly McPeak and Elaine Youngs at the Hellas Open. Misty and Kerri's streak of 14 consecutive tournaments breaks Karch Kiraly/Kent Steffes and Greg Lee/Jim Menges record of 13.

Shelda Bede and Adriana Behar get the most wins in the history of beach volleyball by a women's team with their 31st victory together in the Japan Open.

In 2005, Adriana Behar, with her bronze medal finish at the Swiss Open in Gstaad, becomes the first woman ever in the history of beach volleyball to top one million dollars in FIVB career winnings.

2

VOLLEYBALL: SKILLS AND TECHNIQUES

The game of Volleyball is a dandy game and more besides. At its top level competitive aspect, it is a fast moving energetic game demanding skill, strength, agility, team work and intelligence from its players. At its lowest level, it is an enjoyable, easily set-up game from which youngsters and beginners of all ages can quickly gain pleasure and satisfaction. Moreover, both men and women, boys and girls, can play together for sheer fun, which after all is the object of playing any game. The game of volleyball is very simple.

With a short period after its origin, this game gained a wide popularity. It's fantastic increase in popularity can be explained by a host of reasons, which are as follows:

Firstly, it is basically a very simple game, which can be played indoors and outdoors, and is therefore suitable for varying seasons and any climate.

Secondly, the playing area required takes up comparatively little space so that play can take place in a gym, a sports hall, the park, the beach and even some more unlikely places.

Thirdly, it can be played by players of both sexes and over a considerable age range.

Fourthly, the equipment required is simple and still relatively inexpensive.

Play can be of tremendously varying standards, from a purely recreative level on the beach and in the park,. through all levels of clubs and school competitions, right up to the supremely demanding and fiercely competitive play at international level.

The way in which the game is played now is a far cry from that designed by William Morgan. Decades of competition have produced increasingly well performed skills and a steady development of new tactics as coaches strive for ever higher standards of play. The rules of the game have been reviewed at regular intervals, with changes made when necessary to try to keep attack and defence well balanced, to produce long, closely fought rallies in order to maintain the game as an exciting spectator sport. The fundamental pattern of the modern game of volleyball is as follows :

The match is played between the two teams of up to twelve players, only six from each team are on court at one time. The game is played on a court which is being divided in two equal parts with the help of a net. Play is started by one player hitting the ball over the net from within the service area behind his own base line. Once the ball passes over the net, the receiving team may hit the ball three times before it must go back over the net.

At international level, competitive teams are supposed to master six basic skills: ***serve, pass, set, spike, block and dig.*** Each of these skills comprise a number of specific techniques that have been introduced along the years and are now considered standard practice in high-level volleyball.

VOLLEYBALL SERVING

All volleyball players should know proper techniques for serving floaters and jump serves. Servers should spend time practicing a pre-serve routine. Developing a routine will help servers focus and be ready to serve.

The basic volleyball techniques for serving are...

1. Toss the ball in front of your serving shoulder.

2. Keep your elbow high and back.

3. Contact the middle of the ball with the middle of your hand.

4. Follow through on your armswing.

These are just guidelines. If you have better success

serving a different way, that's fine, do what works best.

A clean solid contact is key to a good floater. I know when I'm struggling getting a solid contact on my float serve, I'll contact the ball with more of a bent elbow.

I feel this gives me a little more of a window for adjusting to the height of the toss to get that solid contact.

For example, if I were to try and contact the ball with an extend arm every time I serve, the height of my toss would be more critical to getting a good solid contact.

The volleyball serve is the first form of attack. It's the first attempt you have to make a Direct point against the oposite team. You should always serve to make a point or put the oposite team in difficulty.

You will learn quickly that what you do with your feet and lower body determines how well you will perform all volleyball fundamentals. That's why alot of my advice and tips focus on the correct positioning of your feet and lower body.

Feet

In order to begin the serve we first start with your feet positioning. Right handers place your right foot behind your left foot so your Right foot is perpendicular to your Left. Your left foot should be pointed Exactly in the direction of where you want to serve.

If you want to serve down the line then your Left foot, hips and upper body should be pointed straight ahead. When serving cross court your left foot , hips and upper body should be turned and facing cross court. All your body weight should be on your back (right foot. The only lower body movement needed when you serve will be a shift in weight from your back (Right) foot to the front (Left) foot.

Upper Body - Left Arm

Extend your Left arm straight out in front of your palm facing up. Place ball in the palm of this hand.

Toss

The toss is one of the most important elements of the serve. Make sure the starting position for your Left arm is straight out in front of you - not down by your waist. With a straight Left arm Toss the ball no more than 2 feet in the air.

For practice, while learning, let the ball fall to the ground. A correctly tossed ball will land about 10-12 inches - Every Time.

Your toss should be the same EVERY TIME. Two feet up in the air and 10 inches in front of your LEFT foot. If you Toss to the left or right of your front foot

1. you will be forced off balance.

2. you will be forced to chase your toss - which will force you Not to serve in the direction you want to. Believe it or not the TOSS is where many serving errors start.

Right Arm

Right arm is fully extended with fingertips and palm facing downward lightly covering the top of the ball. After the toss - you step forward shifting your body weight from back foot to front foot to meet the ball. At this moment you begin your arm swing.

Start your RIGHT arm swing by pulling your arm straight back - palm facing outward - keep elbow high your elbow should pass Over the level of your ear - in slow motion you should be able to turn your head slightly to look underneath your elbow as you pull your arm back - use.

VOLLEYBALL SERVING STRATEGIES

In the long run, volleyball coaches know which players are the most successful servers. These players produce the most points per serving rotation. There are many strategies for volleyball serving. Volleyball players should explore the many different styles of serving - top spin, floaters, jump serve.Volleyball Serving Topspin

Topspin Serving Techniques

The topspin volleyball serve is a great serve for catching your opponent offguard.

An effective topspin serve moves rapidly across the net dropping quickly to the floor.

The force used to generate the topspin is created by...

1. The postition of the hand when contacting the ball and

2. The follow through

Here are some volleyball coaching cues for teaching the topspin volleyball serve...

1. Lean backward prior to contact

2. Toss the ball higher than you would when serving a float serve

3. Contact the ball in a direct line with the hitting shoulder

4. Hit the bottom third of the volleyball

5. Snap your wrist. Your hand should go up and back over the ball.

6. Transfer your bodyweight from the back foot to the front foot during the movement.Volleyball Serving Floater

Float Serve Techniques

Like many other volleyball skills, a key to becoming a great server is executing perfect repetition.

When learning the float serve, you want to keep it simple. The more movement you have when executing this skill, the more likely you are to make an error.

It's important the arms comes straight back with the ball being tossed in front of the hitting arm.

The Toss

A poor toss is often the single big factor to poor serving

Coaching Tips for Serving.

Begin the serve with the player standing in a stride stance.

Place a marker on the floor marking where the tossed ball should land. This spot should be one step in front of the serving arm. Player should practice for awhile tossing the ball and letting the ball drop.

The Draw

The movement of the hitting arm is often referred to as the draw. As the player tosses the ball, the hitting arm draws back with the elbow high.

The hand should be opened up as if you were to high five. The arm then comes forward almost like a throwing motion with the elbow leading the hand to contact the ball.

A poor toss usually results in a poor draw. Have the players practice by tossing the ball, drawing back then catching the ball.

Contact Point

The contact point for the volleyball floater should be where the middle of the hand meets the middle of the ball.

It's best to have a strong open hand when contacting the ball. The wrist shouldn't be bent, it should be inline with the forearm.

Contacting the ball in a spot other than right in the center of the ball will likely cause some spin which then results in a non-knuckle ball effect.

Volleyball Serving Tough, Keys to Successful Serving

Strategies for becoming a good server

1. You must practice serving. You become a better server by practicing your serving. The more you practice, the more experience you develop. Experience and repetition are key. Like a basketball player shooting free throws or an American football placekicker practicing kicking field goals, the skills are developed with repetition.

2. Develop a preserve routine. Your serving technique and mechanics should be the same with every repetition.

3. Serve against passers. It is much more game like to serve with opponents passing. You can tell a lot by how effective your serve is when you are up against passers trying to pass your serves.

4. Practice serving under pressure. Serving in a game is much different than serving in practice when there's no pressure. In practice create games or drills that have some sort of pressure applied. This will also have the added benefit of making the practices more constructive because players will be forced to focus more.

VOLLEYBALL PASSING

Common volleyball techniques for great passing include...

1. Keep your body's center of gravity level when moving. Basically, you want to be light on your feet when getting in position to pass.

2. Being able to take steps without bouncing off the ground is important because it's harder to focus on the ball when you're bouncing up and down.

3. Strong eccentric quadriceps strength leads to a better ability to absorb the force from the ground when

taking steps.

4. Form a solid platform with your forearms. Extend your arms while locking your elbows and turning your hands down at the wrists. You want to form a solid

platform that provides stability.

5. Use your hips and legs to pass, not the arms. Being able to move quickly into position is very important.

6. Concentrate on getting into a stable position quickly, everytime you pass. If you utilize this technique every time you pass, with repetition you will train yourself to be a better passer.

7. If you don't have very good movement skills or are just lazy when moving to pass, you'll have to adjust your

technique on the fly which will lead to fewer consistent passes.

Volleyball techniques for overhead passing with your hands. If you are going to take the ball with your hands to pass, it is usually easier to pass by using a quick finger action to direct the ball to your target.

This quick finger action (sometimes multiple contacts of the fingers) allows for better control. Only do this on the first team contact because on the second and third contact, multiple contacts are illegal.

This works real well for balls that are hard driven or are really far way from your target.

On balls that come right over the net or fall to you pretty slowly, it may be easiest to just take the ball like you normally would with your hands(your normal setting motion).

VOLLEYBALL SETTING

Volleyball techniques for setting consists of the following steps...

1. Get to the target. The second ball is always the setters. Seeing as though they know this ahead of time, setters should be lined up properly and ready to move to the target.

2. Be ready to move from the target. If possible, take your first step directly to where the ball is being passed.

3. The better judgment the setter has, the better job they will do in moving straight to where the ball is going.

4. If they leave too early or they make a bad judgment, they'll step in the wrong direction and not make it there

as quickly.

5. Beat the ball to the spot. Setters should try anticipating where the ball is going to be passed. By paying attention to how tough the serve is and watching the way their passer is handling the ball, they may get a good read on the pass.

6. Stop and set. Everything done up until now dictates how well the setter is able to stop and set.

VOLLEYBALL ATTACKING

Develop consistent footwork. Volleyball techniques for the approach consist of 3 or 4 foot steps. The 3 step approach would be, left-right-left for right handed attackers, right-left-right for left handed attackers. Before training players to develop a consistent 4 step approach or 3 step approach, it may be best to first work on just the last two steps.

Your last two steps are the ones that matter the most. First concentrate on learning the last two before working on 3 or 4 step approaches.

Volleyball techniques for executing an attack hit include...

1. Approaching quick. To jump high, you've got to move fast. Really focus on stepping quickly (especially the last couple) in order to maximize your jump height.

2. Swing your arms back. By swinging your arms back you will take advantage of elastic energy and your nervous systems stretch reflex which can add inches to your vertical.

3. Bring both your arms up. By bring both your arms up you will continue with the momentum of going up which will help maximizing your height. Also, you will be in a better body position to hit.

4. Contact the ball in front of your hitting shoulder. It's best to contact the ball at the same spot every time you hit. This develops a consistent armswing.

5. Volleyball techniques of a hitters footwork (jumping from the correct spot) have a big influence on you hitting the ball in your sweet spot.

6. Put top-spin on the ball. Being able to put top-spin

on the ball when you hit allows you to have better angles when hitting, thus more court to hit into.

This is often called snapping the wrist when contacting the ball.

VOLLEYBALL BLOCKING

Volleyball techniques for blocking involve learning to see the court and making quick decisions at the net when preparing to block.

Having good court vision involves making good judgments while watching the setter, the ball, and hitters.

Good court vision. You often can predict where the setter is going to set the ball by watching the ball after it's passed.

The better you are able to judge where the ball is being passed, the better you can predict what the setter is going to do with it.

Watching the setter and hitters is critical to getting in the best position to block.

Identify the front row players. All the blockers should know who the front row players are before the serve.

Also, identify the setter as front row or back row to know if the setter can legally attack the second ball.

The volleyball techniques shuffle and crossover step are used to move into optimal blocking position.

Shuffle step. The shuffle technique is probably easiest because the hips stay square to the net.

Crossover step. The crossover is harder because you turn your hips during the movement and you need to get squared back up to the net before you jump.

The crossover is better for when you have to travel far to get in position to block because you can get there faster than shuffling.

Jump straight up, and penetrate the net. Blockers need good balance and stability to develop a consistent block jump.

The better a blocker is at jumping up and not floating, the better they will be at staying out of the net and penetrating their block into the opponent's space.

Wide fingers and thumbs up when blocking. Keep the

fingers spread wide and tight and thumbs pointing up to prevent jamming your fingers.

Spreading your fingers wide will also allow you to take up more space.

Volleyball techniques for your blocking hands.Angle your hands to block the ball into your opponents court. The outside blocker should reach and penetrate a little more with the outside hand.

This will give that outside hand a little better angle for blocking the ball into the court and not out of bounds. If you're confident you won't block the ball back out of bounds, it's always a good idea to surround the ball with your hands when blocking.

VOLLEYBALL DIGGING

Start in a defensive position lined up around the block. Know what area your blockers are going to take up (line or angle).

The basics of volleyball techniques for digging...

1. Be up on your toes and on the

balls of your feet, not on your heels.

2. Be ready to get in a stable position to dig a hard driven ball.

3. Be ready to move to run down a shot or tip.

4. Arms are bent and in front of you ready to react to dig a ball with your forearms or to play a ball overhead.

5. Eyes are focused on the hitter watching for any hint as to what they are going to do.

6. Cushion hard driven balls. You should try to absorb the hit with your arms to keep the ball on your side of the net.

7. If you can keep the ball on your side, your team has a better chance of winning the rally with your setter setting an attacker.

8. Volleyball techniques for going to the floor. Players are encouraged to stay on their feet when making plays on the ball.

9. For making emergency plays, there are five common techniques...

10. Collapse. From a low defensive position, a player might collapse to the ground in order to make a last second move to play the ball. The collapse is used most often when a ball falls shorter than anticipated.

11. Sprawl. Anticipating the ball falling out in front of them, a defender might use the sprawling technique to take a lunge forward and reach to make a play.

12. Sprawling volleyball techniques are just like the collapse except the defender has time to take a step and reach.

The dive. This is similar to the sprawl except the body is more in an airborne position when making a the play.

Pancake. Defensive players can perform a pancake to save a ball from hitting the floor. The pancake is similar to a sprawl except the fingers are spread firmly and placed on the ground to meet the ball.

Pancaking can be one of the good volleyball techniques of playing a ball because if you perform a good pancake, you often will get a good bounce that will allow your teammates to keep the ball in play.

Shoulder or barrel roll. Defenders can often use a rolling technique by extending to the right, left, or forward in attempting to get the ball up by playing the ball close to the floor.

After playing the ball the players use their momentum to roll over their body and regain their balance in a position ready to move.

Rolling is probably the safest of the emergency volleyball techniques because players don't really hit the ground hard.

VOLLEYBALL SERVE BASIC

The volleyball serve is the only skill in volleyball where the player has complete control over proper execution.

1. With a tough serve, a player can for a point immediately (serving an ace).

2. With a tough serve, a player can force the opponent to return the ball back over the net in an easy manner (free ball).

It's important to not take serving for granted. If a player

has a "just serve in" attitude, they are missing a golden opportunity to put their team to the advantage.

Especially if the opponent sides out effectively, you need to give your team the advantage if you can. As teams advance in skills and tactics serving becomes even more important.

It's much different to serve in practice than when actually serving in a game situation win a match or tournament could be on the line. Therefore, volleyball serving drills should be created to give players game like pressure.

Types of Volleyball Serves

The main types of volleyball serves are the underhand, float, and topspin serves.

The underhand serve is the type of serve most beginning players learn first. It's also common for coaches to initiate drills with the underhand serve.

The float serve is probably the møst common type of volleyball serve. It's called a foat serve because it's served with the purpose of the ball floating around making it hard for the opponent to pass.

The topspin serve is the least common serve. Topspin serves can be very effective if developed. Topspin serves can dropped quickly in front of the opponent making in extremely difficult to pass. Also, deep topspin serves are tough because the ball may appear to be going out of bounds then at the last second drop in the court.

Underhand Volleyball Serving

Techniques for the Underhand Serve

The underhand serve is the easiest serve to teach because there are so few variables. Since the serve doesn't involve a toss it's much easier to learn and control.

Tips for the Underhand Serve

1. Start in a stride position with the weight on the back foot.

2. (This is the position for a right handed server.) Hold the ball in the left hand in front of your body just below the waist and in front of the right hip.

3. Slightly lean forward.

4. The eyes should be focused on the ball where contact is going to be made.

5. Swing the arm back and then forward contacting the ball with the palm of the hand.

6. Weight is transfered to the front foot while contacting the ball facing the intended direction the served ball is going.

7. The left hand drops just before contacting the ball.

8. After contact the serving arm follows through toward the intended target.

Float Volleyball Serves

Techniques for Serving Floaters

Float serves are real effective for when the opposing passers don't keep their eyes on the ball. Floaters keep the passers on their toes ready to react to the changes in the flight of the ball.

Float serves allow the ball to move up, down, left or to the right making it more difficult for passers to judge where the ball is traveling.

When tossing the ball, the maximum height of the ball should be. about slightly higher than the player's maximum reach. As the player makes contact, the hand should pop off the ball. The ball should be struck hard. The ball should be contacted in the center. A firm contact in the middle of the ball is what creates the floating action.

Starting Position

Start by standing with your upper body facing the

direction you are going to serve the ball. Place the feet so that it will be easy to rotate the upper body easily through a throwing type motion.

For a right handed server start with the left foot forward with the right foot pointed outward to the right.

The ball is held in the opposite hand ready to toss.

Small Step and Toss

For some players, drawing the arm back takes longer than tossing the ball. So you may want to start drawing the arm back before you toss.

For serving floaters, the toss is out in front of the body, contacting the ball without it dropping significantly. Take a small step with your left foot (assuming you're right handed) and at the same time transfer your body weight in the direction you are serving.

Striking the Center of the ball

To serve an effective floater, the ball should be contacted firmly by your hands palm. A good solid contact in the center of the ball allows for the ball to be served without spin. The goal should be to serve the ball without putting spin on it which helps to create a knuckle ball action which allows the ball to dance in the air making it much more difficult to pass. Beginning players may practice dragging the back foot when serving. By dragging the back foot, this helps remind players to only step with the front foot.

Tips for Serving Floaters

1. Upper body facing the direction you're serving. Left foot is in front.

2. Draw the hitting hand back keeping the elbow up and back.

3. Take a small step as you toss the ball.

4. Contact the ball in the center.

5. Drag the back foot.

Topspin Volleyball Serve

A big difference between the topspin and floater is the follow through.

To hit an effective topspin, the ball must also be contacted a little more back and up.

You should toss the ball ball over your hitting shoulder forcing you to step under the ball.

The ball should be contacted using a wrist snapping action. Wrist snapping helps put topspin on the ball.

The speed and power that can be generated helps as an encentive for players to develop a good topspin serve.

Good topspin serves can be real effective because passers rarely see them. The dropping movement on topspin serves can catch lazy passers out of position and not ready to pass.

Why are Volleyball Players so Lean?

Have you ever wondered why volleyball players are so lean and have great muscle definition? The short answer is volleyball involves a lot of jumping and quick/ hard sprints. In volleyball, there are about 5 to 15 seconds between plays. So basically, it's like doing interval training with tons and tons of sprints and jumps. As you might know, interval training is the best form of training for weight loss and getting real lean. This is especially why beach volleyball players are so lean. Beach players have to quickly sprint and jump high out of sand. This is much more demanding than playing indoor volleyball. The same way sprinters are much more lean than most long distance runners, volleyball players are also leaner due to interval-type of conditioning and resistance training programs. Volleyball players burn more fat after those type of workouts compared to the most "steady-state" aerobic workouts.

Volleyball Alignment and Overlapping

At the moment of serve contact, players need to be in the right volleyball alignment with no overlapping of adjacent players. Adjacent players are ones front to back or side to side. In the diagram above, the arrows show which two players the player in zone 1 can't overlap. RB is zone 1 (Right Back), RF is zone 2 (Right Front), CF is zone 3 (Center Front), LF is zone 4 (Left Front), LB is zone 5 (Left Back), and CB is zone 6 (Center Back). RB must be properly aligned with RF and CB. RF must be properly aligned with CF and RB. CF must be properly aligned with CB, LF, and RF. LF must be properly aligned with LB and CF. LB must be properly aligned with LF and CB. CB must be properly aligned with CF, LB, and RB. The diagram above shows legal alignment. This is a typical alignment for a setter that is in zone 1. The setter pushes the zone 2 player to the net. Players in zone 3 and 4 back up to help out with passing. You can see none of the adjacent players are overlapping. Avoiding Overlaps Consider the position of the players foot relative to the feet of the adjacent player. Only consider the foot or feet touching the floor. The right side player must have at least part of one foot closer to the right sideline than both feet of the center player in the corresponding row (except the server and the center back of the serving team). The left side player must have at least part of one foot closer to the left sideline than both feet of the center player in the corresponding row. Each front row player must have at least one part of one foot closer to the centerline than both feet of the corresponding back row player. Players can move prior to serve. Players can have their foot touching the boundary line during the serve. At the moment of serve contact, no part of the body can be touching outside the boundary lines. After the contact for serve, players can move to whatever position on the court they want to.

Mental Volleyball Training

Have you ever felt like you were playing in the zone. When you're in this ideal performance state, there is an absense of negative self talk and a strong feeling of efficacy. An important aspect is that the athlete trusts

in their skills and conditioning level and they just "let it happen" without interference from negative thoughts.

Case Study 1: --------- "I'm Dr. Jekyll and Mr. Hyde when it comes to football. When I'm on the field sometimes I don't know what I am doing out there. People ask me about this move or that move, but I don't know why I did something, I just did it. I am able to focus out the negative things around me and just zero in on what I am doing out there. Off the field I become myself again." – Walter Payton, a premiere running back in NFL history - --------- Characteristics of players being in the zone... a sense of effortlessness - an involuntary experience absence of fear - no fear of failure a narrow focus of attention concentrated on the activity itself no thinking about or analysis of performance a distortion of time and space, in which time seems to slow a sense of personal control The following are 7 factors that go into you playing in the zone. These 7 factors work together collectively producing the excellence you desire to win at volleyball. What do you see? The first one has to to with what you see. Ask yourself what you see when you are experiencing being in the zone. These factors are important because they trigger your mind to get you into the state of mind you want it to be in so you can play the best you're capable of... playing volleyball in the zone. How do you feel? What does it feel like to be in the zone? If you are able to repeat this feeling when you play volleyball, it's much easier to get in the zone. What are you saying to yourself? What's your inner communication? Pay attention to what you're saying to yourself. It's unlikely your self talk is negative or you wouldn't be in the zone. Pay attention to the conversation that's going on inside your head when you're in the zone and compare that to the conversation that's going on when you're out of the zone. Then, when you are not in the zone, you can start talking to yourself as if you were, then that will trigger the right mindset, then you can get back in the zone. What are you expecting? Ask yourself before you play what you expect is going to happen. How do you expect to play? What you expect is much different when you're in the zone. For instance, if you don't expect to play well, you can't get in the zone. When you're in the zone, you are confident and you can make plays easily and more effortless. Carry the same facial expressions. What facial expressions do you make when you're in the zone? Mimicking the same expressions can make it much easier to get in the zone. What visual scenarios do you have going on inside your mind when you're in the zone? You want to reflect the same mental thoughts and images you have in your mind. This will trigger your subconscious mind to help you play at your highest ability. How do you breathe? How you breathe when you're in the zone is different than when you aren't. It's common for athlete's to describe being in the zone as an imobilizing calmness. How do you breathe when you are playing your best? Is your heart racing? Are you relaxed? You should ask yourself these questions. Many players and coaches make the mistake of not considering the mental side of volleyball training. Having the ability to put yourself in the right state of mind can give you a big advantage to succeeding in volleyball.

QUICK REVIEW OF VOLLEYBALL SKILLS AND TECHNIQUES

SERVICE

Service is the easiest skill to learn. Though largely a

matter of physical ability, the importance of precision and dependability should be stressed. Untempered strength results in many mistakes.

Service is the putting of ball into play. First player hits the ball with one hand, open or closed or any part of the arm, to send it over the net into the opponents' court.

A consistent serve is important because only the serving team can score. The serve has an expected success rate that is 80 to 90 per cent higher than the other skills because the server tosses the ball to himself rather than receiving the ball from other player.

Equally important is the fact that serve is the first opportunity a team has to put the opponent at a disadvantage.

Stand or step and stride with the foot opposite the striking arm. That lead foot is positioned 2 feet in front of the back foot and is pointed directly toward the intended target. The stride starts as the ball is tossed into the air. The toss is made in front of the striking shoulder and at contact is in front of the striding body parallel with the front foot. The ball is tossed low for controlled accuracy.

A two-handed spin free toss aids accuracy. The striking arm action on the toss resembles an overhand throwing motion. As the ball is released on the toss, the arms flexes, the elbow draws back at shoulder height, and the upper body rotates so that the non-striking shoulder is in a leading position and the alignment of both shoulders is approximately 45 degrees with the back line of the court. The elbow snaps forward ahead of the wrist, and forearm accelerates in preparation for ball contact.

The wrist of the striking arm is tense and locked, the hand is open wide, presenting a flat contact surface, and the ball is aggressively contacted with the bottom half of the hand at a point slightly higher than head level. Velocity is generated by the elbow snap throwing the forearm forward, and the ball accelerates rapidly as it is contacted with the hard surface of the hand. Body weight transfers to the front foot, and the forearm of the striking arm is immediately stopped at contact, producing a recoil action. Body balance is maintained as both feet remain in contact with the floor and all movement is directly at the target on the follow-through.

UNDERARM SERVICE

Underarm services are the easiest to perform. There are two types, the frontal and the lateral. For the first, the player stands square to the net, his left foot forward if he is right-handed, legs slightly bent. If he is right-handed, he holds the ball in his left hand, his right arm held slightly behind him, hand cupped and fingers pressed together. As the ball leaves his left hand, his striking arm swings forward. His hand hits the lower back part of the ball, in front of him at waist-height.

At the same time, he straightens his front leg and trunk, bringing his back leg forwards and moving into position on court. He must avoid the following mistakes:

- placing his feet wrongly;
- his striking arm being too bent;
- hitting the ball either too near or too far from his body.

The second type of underarm service, the lateral service, is made from almost the same stance, but the player stands with his shoulders perpendicular to the net. The striking arm swings forward across the body. The action is practised in the same way as the other type of underarm serve.

OVERARM SERVICE

There are four types of overarm service, which are as follows:

-strong tennis serve,

-the floating tennis serve,

-the strong windmill serve; and

-the floating windmill serve.

Nowadays the strong services are rarely used, due to

the high proportion of mistakes that they entail, even when performed by the most experienced players. Most team therefore use the floating service almost exclusively. They are very much more consistent and in the end, are more effective.

Tennis Serve—For the strong tennis service, the player

begins from a well-balanced position, with one foot in front of the other and the shoulders parallel to the net. As he throws, the ball in the air, his striking arm swings behind his head, elbow held high, hand cupped and shoulders turned away from the net. Then his weight swings forward. He hits the ball at a foot. His back leg swings forward as he hit the ball, so that he is already moving to take up his position on court.

Floating Tennis Serve—The player adopts the same initial position for a floating tennis service. The serve is made without effort and without using the trunk. The ball is hit centrally, with the heel of the hand. The hand may be either open or closed. The arm and hand action is halted abruptly at the moment the ball is hit. The main objective is to avoid making the ball spin, if it spins it will not float in the air.

Strong Windmill Serve—The strong windmill serve is more difficult to master. The inial stance is the same as for the lateral underarm serve. As he throws, the ball in the air, the player swings his trunk and back leg sideways and, turning away from the court, leans down and extends his serving arm.

From this point, his arm swings up and his whole body straightens. He hits the ball at a point above his head and in front of his body, with the full force of the windmill action. The windmill service depends largely on the ball being thrown up correctly. If the ball is thrown too near to the body or too far to one side or in front, the arm-swing and the positions of the body will automatically change. The ball will then be hit incorrectly.

If the throw is wrong, it is better to let the ball fall, without touching it, and start again. Since this service is difficult, the action should first be practised without the ball. The player should then practise the throw. If the ball is thrown correctly, it should fall on the ground should then be practised by aiming at a ball that is hung at the right height from the ceiling.

If this cannot be arranged, another player can stand on a chair and hold the ball. Great attention should be paid to the correct swing of the arm, and the straightening of the trunk and legs. Later, the player should practise serving at a wall, aiming at different heights, from a distance of 5 to 7 metres. After this, the player can serve over the net, at first from about 4 metres away and then gradually increasing the distance. The strength of the service is of no importance until the action has been properly learned.

Floating Windmill Service—This is usually known as the Japanese serve, is one of the most common in the modern game. It is normally performed from the same initial stance as the strong windmill serve, although there are many different individual styles.

A study of the Japanese national women's team showed that the players had their own individual ways of performing the service. The most common method is as follows, from the initial stance, the player almost turns his back to the net. Even the hand holding the ball is behind the body, towards the side of the striking arm. As the body straightens, the player throws the ball much lower and nearer to the body than in the strong windmill serve.

At the same time, the other arm loosely extended and the rest of the body swing quickly on to the ball. The impact is relatively slight. The ball is usually hit with the flat of the hand but, as with the tennis floater, there is no follow through and the ball is hit so that it does not spin.

A player has to spend a great deal of time practising service, if his serve is to be precise, consistent and attacking. To help maintain the players' interest, anything from five form of a competition.

Several services, anything from five to fifty, can be made in succession, with a system of points in operation. At the same time, to keep the players under pressure physically, so that they are serving in conditions similar to a match, they can be asked to volley, to change direction, to dive or to block between services. If this is not done, the situation is unreal since service alone requires very little physical exertion.

Tactics on Service

Service has become a weapon of attack and its tactical use is important. Generally speaking, its object is not to score points directly, but to make it more difficult for the opposition to organise an effective attack. Only the team with service is able to score points. This team tries to retain service and scores points for as long as it does on.

On losing service, a team must make every possible effort to regain it. The brief moment before service is used by each team to organise its line-up. There follows an account of serving tactics and systems of service reception. Given the importance of retaining service, the player who serves without thinking and makes a real gift to his opponents must be condemned.

Although service constitutes an attack, the only other five players in the serving team prepare to defend. The success of this defence will largely depend on the service. If the service succeeds in putting pressure on the opposition, it is likely that they will make an easy return, which then allows the serving team to build an effective counter-attack. The server must adopt certain principles which are as follows:

-aim for consistency and precision rather than use any type of service whose only advantage is strength. Generally speaking, the more powerful the service, the less it is precise and the more likely to make a fault;

-always aim at the weak point in the opposition's line-up, or at the players whose reception is the least good;

-seek out the tension that is often felt by players receiving service, continue to serve at a player who has already made a mistake, serve at a player who has been substituted on court and has not yet touched the ball;

-use any exterior factors which might help, the

lighting or draughts indoors, the sun or the wind out-of-doors,

-as soon as he has served, the server must move quickly to his position in the defensive line-up.

VOLLEYBALL OVERHAND SERVE TECHNIQUE

The following steps should be followed to learn overhead service in volleyball:-

1. If you are a right handed person do the following steps. If you are a lefty do the opposite of those steps that say to use your right leg or arm.

2. Line up both of your feet about shoulder distance apart with your right foot ahead of your left. Your shoulders and hips should be aligned with the net.

3. Put your arms straight in front of you (do not bend your arms)

4. Hold the bottom of the ball with the palm of your left hand and the top with the palm of your right hand (your elbows and arms shouldn't touch any other part of your body).

5. Cock your serving arm back next to your head and make sure your elbow is pointing upwards and then toss the ball up with your palm of your left hand (not fingers) about 2-3 feet in the air, step forward with your left foot, and hit the bottom of the ball with the palm of your right hand (this will give it spin causing it to go higher and farther). Your hand should be stiff and open and your wrist straight. Make sure your serving hand is aiming in a slanted up position, this way the ball will go higher and make it over the net. if you aim down with your hand, the ball will hit the ground before it goes over the

net. Also, make sure you are hitting the ball at its highest point when you throw it in the air, if you hit the ball on the way down, the outcome will not be very good. Do not throw the ball very high!

6. After striking the ball use your momentum and run to your defensive position.

7. Think of these steps in your head when you serve, toss, step, hit and follow through.

Tips

1. Perfect your underhand serve first, so if you have a bad overhand serving day, you are always confident with that!

2. Practice makes precision(not perfection!), so practice this a lot!

3. Try different variations to the above steps; DIFFERENT THINGS WORK FOR DIFFERENT PEOPLE!

4. Don't punch the ball ("shot put"), swing at it.

5. If you're having trouble with your serve, try practicing just the toss. If you throw it up and just let it drop, it should land directly in front of your right foot, which should still be in the position in front of your right foot, before the step. Practice this fifty times a day and your serve should seriously improve.

6. Using your momentum can help a lot especially if you have a small body. Really just whail on the ball. You need a lot of strength to get your serve over the net.

7. If you feel like you would be more comfortable taking a few steps or jumping while serving, you should try a jump serve.

8. Make sure not to "slap" the ball. Hit it hard with the palm of your hand.

9. Get comfortable with how the ball will go where you toss it. For example, when you toss the ball far out in front, the ball will travel flat. In order to serve a nice loopy, short ball, toss the ball a little closer to your shoulder. Balls that drop inside the 3-meter line is extremely deadly for the opposing team.

10. You should be able to hear a solid thud when you hit the ball if it is a good serve.

11. Make sure you follow through, sometimes if you don't the ball may travel a different direction.

12. Taking a big step will really increase the power of your serve.

13. If you are having trouble, ask a coach or older, more skilled volleyball player to help you and critique your serve.

14. It may take a while to get your serve over, in the long run it'll work out and you're serve will be deadly

15. For stronger serving work on your chest shoulders and triceps, strength in these muscles can be gained by doing pushups

16. If you can't 'slap' the ball and get it over the net, try using your fist. Toss the ball up, and instead of slapping it, make a fist and pound the ball.

17. If you do use your fist, make sure you hit it with the front part of the fist. In other words, hold your hand like you would slap the ball, but curl your fingers

18. If you have ever played tennis before the serves

are fairly similar and have the same set up process.

Remember: if you think that you tossed it up badly, LET IT DROP. In a real game, you are allowed to let the ball drop once.

Also when playing volleyball always remember that you don't have to be afraid of diving for the ball,but don't do it unless needed otherwise you will give the other team points.

Try not to worry and think too much about getting it over the net the first couple of times you try it. Get your technique down before worring about getting it over.

Once you toss the ball up in the air, don't reach for the ball. Wait for it to fall at the right moment so you can hit it.

Practice your underhand serves and then go to overhand. If you can't do an underhand serve, you probably aren't strong enough, for an overhand! The overhand takes time to get it 100% Right!

PASSING

Tips on Passing

1. Whenever you are called upon to pass, you must first get into position, which means getting the ball between your knees, and contacting it at about

zipper level.

2. Then, you must bend your knees. Don't bend at the waist. Bending at the knees allows you to keep your eyes up, so you can see what's going on.

The key to good volleyball skills for effective passing is being in an athletic posture ready to react and move every second the ball is in play.

Ready Stance

Players should start in an athletic position relaxed and ready to move. Stand with your knees flexed comfortably with your weight on the balls of your feet.

React and Move

- Footwork must be quick and aggressive to allow time to get in front of the ball to pass.
- Your first step should be with the foot that is closest to the ball. When moving, your head should not bounce. It is to your advantage to arrive early to play the ball.

• The earlier you are, the more time you have to make quick adjustments to your foot positions.

Track the Ball

• As a passer, it's best to track the ball from the time it leaves the servers hand to the time it reaches your arms.

• Pay attention to how the server contacts the ball and how the ball moves as it comes to your side of the court.

• Look to see if the ball is spinning or floating to help get a read on where the ball is going to end up.

Develop a Rhythm and Flow to Passing

• Develop the habit of reacting as soon as you know where the ball is going.

• A lot of players wait too long and end up struggling to get into position to pass.

Volleyball Skills for Forearm Passing

Three techniques for forearm passing...

Midline

It is best to get your body directly behind the ball and pass the ball from the midline of your body. Your body should be facing your target while taking a small step with either foot while passing.

Angle Right

The angle right technique is used when a player gets behind the ball and passes to the target that's to their right. This ball is taken outside the frame of the body while dropping the right shoulder.

or passing an easy free ball.

• Feet should be spread with the hips, shoulders, and knees square facing your target.

• The fingers and hands should push straight through when playing the ball. Having the hands firm and close together helps you control the ball.

• Players being served deep can use this technique by starting midcourt and then taking a step back as they take the ball.

• Front row players can use the overhand technique to take short serves with their hands rather than being force to pass with their forearms.

First Ball, Double Contact

Since it is legal to have multiple contacts in a single attempt to play the ball on a teams first contact, coaches are utilizing volleyball skills for overhand passing more than ever. Some coaches even teach players to pass this ball with their fingers quickly to avoid being called for a lift.

Deciding whether to teach passing overhead or with

the forearms is often difficult. By teaching multiple passing techniques players are given the opportunity to develop their own unique passing strategies and techniques.

HAND SET

No matter how your body and hands are positioned, your volleyball skills for setting should be consistent. That is, your hand technique for playing the ball should be the same every time you attempt to set.

Volleyball Skills for Learning to Hand Set

Learning hand position for setting...

1. With your hands down in front of you, put all ten fingertips together (thumbs touching each other, index fingers touching each other, etc.) with the fingers spread wide.

2. Raise your hands up above your head with your fingers still touching.

3. Pull your elbows out to your sides.

4. Pull your hands apart just far enough so that a ball fits between them.

Contacting the Ball

The fingers are the only part of your hand that touches the ball, never the palms. Your thumbs, index fingers, and middle fingers are what you use with your wrists to catch and push the ball.

The little fingers and ring finger just give you extra control when setting.

Volleyball skills progressions for developing clean

hands...

1. Catch

Toss the ball to yourself, then just catch the ball with your hands in the correct position.

2. Catch and Push

Catch a ball in the correct position. After a pause, continue through a setting motion.

3. Shorter and Shorter Pauses

Concentrate on catching the ball with correct hand positions and gradually make the pauses shorter. As

you're setting, focus on taking spin off the ball.

Volleyball Skills for Getting in Position to Set

The best setter's move in a direct line to the ball and deliver the set efficiently to the hitter.

Setters should explode to the ball; arrive early with the hands up.

Correct volleyball skills footwork for moving from the target position...

1. Left-Right-Left

When you're at the target waiting for the pass, have your bodyweight on your right foot ready to take a step with your left in the direction of the passed ball.

2. Big Right, Then Left

If you have accurate passers, a setter can get into position quicker by taking a big right step to the spot the ball is being passed. After that big step, pivot squaring up to the left antennae.

Even if you are slow, you can still develop good footwork to get to the ball faster than other setters with poor technique.

Volleyball skills for Pursuing the Ball

Setters should emphasize getting to the ball first before focusing on setting technique.

If you can't run and get to the ball quickly and efficiently, setting the ball is going to be much more difficult. A common mistake beginning setter's make is running after a ball with their hands up in the air.

Although I agree you should get your hands up early

ready to set, you should use your arms first to move to the ball.

Volleyball Skills for Squaring Up

The best way to develop consistent sets is facing your target every time. A good rule of thumb is to always face the left antennae when setting.

Use both your arms and legs to guide the ball and follow through with both hands pointing towards the target.

Volleyball Skills for Setting

Good setter's often make attackers look good just from being able to deliver consistent sets.

Setting High Outside

Setters need to really concentrate on contacting a ball cleanly when setting high outside. The farther the ball needs to travel, the more likely you are to double contact with your hands.

With sets that travel a greater distance, referees have more time to decide on calling hands because...

1. There is a longer hand contact on the ball.

2. The ball is in the air a longer time, allowing for the referee see the rotation of the ball and think about possibly call the set.

If you're having trouble setting the ball far enough outside, really focus on powerfully extending your arms and hands through to the target.

Setting a Quick Ball

Setting a short quicker set can be done by just using

a quick wrist action. This is best done with a less follow through (or no body extension).

These sets can be easier because there is less body movement. The set is performed mainly by the wrists.

Key Volleyball Skills for Successful Sets

Get to the Ball

1. Get to the ball as quick as you can

2. Square your body up to the target

Setting Position

1. Have your right foot slightly in front with your bodyweight balanced

2. Your shoulders, hips, and feet face the target

3. Knees are bent and your back is straight

4. Hands are above your forehead

5. Hands are in the shape of the ball

Setting Action

1. Contact the ball above the forehead

2. Keep elbows comfortably bent

3. Use your legs to generate power through your body up to your hands

4. Fully extend your arms and then your entire body

It's important to note that no two setter's set the same way. Regardless of your volleyball skills, what's important is that you get the job done.

Therefore, it may be best for player's to experiment with different volleyball strategies for setting to develop their own unique setting technique.

VOLLEYBALL DRILLS FOR HITTING

Hitting volleyball drills are some of the most fun drills players can do to become better at playing volleyball. When first learning how to play volleyball, it's a good idea to train players the correct way to approach, jump, and hit because it's much harder to change habit once it's developed.

Reach and Snap - Hitting Volleyball Drills

The purpose of this volleyball drill is to work on the volleyball skills for the technique in hitting a volleyball.

Players partner up. Players warm up shoulders by throwing the ball back and forth to one another.

After the shoulder warm up, players start tossing the ball up to themselves and hit to each other.

Players focus on reaching high and snapping their wrist when contacting the ball.

Variations Players can first start by just reaching high and snapping. Don't use a follow through arm swing at first. Just work on reaching high and snapping the wrist.

Once players become more comfortable snapping the wrist, they can add in the arm swing.

Also, players can work on bringing both arms up in the air when tossing the ball. So now the player is in more of an attacking position, ready to swing.

Benefits All hitters need to learn to reach high when they hit. If their elbow is bent, they won't hit as high and will be more likely to get blocked. Also, reaching high allows for the hitter to hit more easily around the block. Many players spend hours and hours training to increase their volleyball vertical jump height a couple inches when they could have got those inches by simply changing their arm swing (reaching high).

All hitters should develop a good wrist snap. Perfecting the volleyball spike by snapping the wrist, not only does a hitter hit harder but they also have more court to hit into because they can hit at sharper angles into the court.

Team Approach Jumps - Hitting Volleyball Drills

The purpose of this volleyball drill is to work on the technique for the volleyball spike approach. No volleyballs are needed for this drill.

Have the team form a line along a sideline. The first player in line takes an approach to the net. After the approach, the player backs off the net and then takes another approach. This time, the approach starts from a little farther inside the court. The player repeats this until they reach the other sideline.

After the first player volleyball approaches to the net, the next player follows. This continues until all the player reach the other sideline.

Variations Players can emphasize proper footwork. For example, players can work on a 4 step volleyball approach. Players can also work on creativity (experiment with steps, for example 3 steps vs. 4 steps) to discover possible volleyball strategies for hitting.

Players can also work on swinging their arms back during each approach.

Benefits This can be done in practice for when coaches want to look at each players footwork while at the same time running a volleyball drill.

Approach Jumps are also good volleyball drills for team warm up for volleyball practices or games.

Game Simulated Hitting - Hitting Volleyball Drills

The purpose of this volleyball hitting drill is to help

players improve their hitting by simulating hitting in game situations.

This drill for volleyball needs six or more players.

The coach tosses the ball over the net to a passer. While the coach is tossing the ball, the players at the net transition off, and the setter penetrates towards the net. The setter then sets the passed ball to any of the three attackers, who then attack the ball.

Players rotate positions after every rally.

The hitters and setter must return to defensive position after every hit.

Benefits This volleyball hitting drill can be used during pre-practice warm up and even part of pre-game warm up.

This volleyball drill is great for setters working on footwork when releasing to the net. This hitter drill is also great for attackers to work on their footwork for transitioning off the volleyball net.

VOLLEYBALL TECHNIQUES FOR ATTACKING

Volleyball skills for attacking consists of 4 parts...

1. The Approach

The purpose of the approach is to position your body in the air ready to hit.

2. The Take-Off

Develop volleyball skills to quickly get off the ground using both legs to jump. The shorter the ground contact time is on the last two steps of the approach the more elastic energy you can utilize for exploding high.

3. The mid-air contact

You want to get positioned with your arm stretched upward about six inches behind the ball, then contact

the ball at your highest point in the jump.

4. The Landing

Cushion your landing by landing on the balls of your feet with your knees bent.

Volleyball Skills for the 4 Step Approach

This is the conventional 4 step approach jump for a right handed hitter.

the order of steps are...

right....left....right-left.

Right Step

The first step is a small step with the right foot. This

step gets you moving.

Left Step

The second step is a bigger and quicker step. You should take this step towards where you think the ball is being set.

Big Right Step and Quick Left

This right step should be taken to place you at the best take-off spot. The left step is taken quickly to help your body transfer your momentum into an explosive jump.

Take Off Spot

Where you jump from the ground is critical to contacting the ball high and in front of the body.

Swinging Arms Back

Attackers should develop the ability to swing their arms down and back as they approach. Attackers should swing their arms back as they are taking their big right step and then bring them up in front of their body as they are jumping.

Volleyball Skills for the 3 Step Approach

the order of steps are...

left....right-left.

The 3 step approach and 4 step approach are basically the same. The only difference is the 3 step approach doesn't have the extra step to help guide you in the right direction. So it may be best to use the 4 step approach if you have a great distance to travel when hitting.

Middle hitters and other attackers that hit quick sets

often use 3 step approaches. The placement for quick sets are more consistent and easier for a hitter to adjust their approaches to.

undamentals of Spiking Volleyball Skills

1. Your arms and hands should be coming up in front of your body as you are jumping.

2. Continue to bring your hands up above your head as you are flying through the air. If you drop either arm you will lose vertical momentum and height.

3. With both arms up, bring your hitting hand back by bending at the elbow.

4. Swing your arm forward making contact with the ball with your arm fully extended.

Volleyball Skills for Effective Attacks

You will often come up against tall players that have developed really good blocking skills. It is to your

1. chase the ball

2. line up with the ball on your hitting shoulder

3. jump off your left foot (if you're right handed)

4. drift through the air as you make contact with the ball

Two methods for a slide approach...

1. Approach at a 45 degree angle to the setter or antennae. The footwork is similar to performing a lay up in basketball.

2. Approach running parallel to the net. If you go parallel the set must be quicker and more accurate because you are closer to the net.

Volleyball skills for hitting slides can be very effective because it's often much easier to adjust your steps and timing than taking an approach jump off two feet.

A slide attack is difficult to defend because...

1. The attacker can hit the ball at various heights and

speeds.

2. It can be difficult to tell where the hitter is going to be set.

3. The hitter can run parallel to the net when approaching which makes it more difficult for blockers and defenders to get in the best position to make a play.

4. Blockers may drift in the direction the hitter is flying which tends to open up holes in the block.

VOLLEYBALL TECHNIQUES FOR BLOCKING

The keys to good blocking volleyball skills are

positioning, timing, and movement.

To be an effective blocker, you need to stay in a balance position ready to anticipate.

Good blocking volleyball skills consists of moving into good position to jump up and penetrate the net with your hands and arms to deflect or block your opponents attack.

Volleyball Skills for Better Footwork

Ready position for blocking...

1. Stand at a comfortable distance off the net. You should be standing with enough leverage to push off and move sideways if you need to.

2. Place your arms up in front of you. You want your arms up ready to react to the other teams offense.

Keep hands up and feet ready to move

You want your hands up rather than at your sides so that you can quickly get them above the net to block. Also, by having your hands up you are less likely to brush your hands with the net as you jump up.

Two step lateral

To perform this move, you basically start by jumping laterally off of one foot. To move to the left, take a big step (or jump) to your left foot. Follow with your right foot, land, and jump straight up.

Two important points...

1. You want to jump lined up in front of where the hitter will be contacting the ball.

2. You want to make sure you are balanced before you jump.

Three step crossover

This is to travel a greater distance sideways at the net. To move left, take a step with your left foot, then cross your right foot over in front of your body (your body is now sideways). After you have planted the right foot, turn and face the net. Jump straight up to block.

Volleyball skills for More Effective Blocking

Practicing blocking is often left out of practice. Players often are left with great potential for improvement. Teams can take over a match with good blocking much like a good server can with their serving.

Court Vision

Know both the setters and hitters tendencies ahead of time. Watch the setter and hitters for clues as to where the setter is going to set and how the attackers are going to approach to hit.

Don't swing your arms

When raising your hands above the net, don't swing your arms towards the net. This will make timing the block even harder. It is also more likely the ball will be hit off of you because your arms may not be in the right place.

Hands position

Your fingers should be spread as wide as possible

when blocking. By spreading them wide you cover more area and help tense them up which makes them stronger for blocking. Strong tense fingers prevents jamming or injuring your fingers during blocking.

Always penetrate the net

Don't try reaching high to block. Instead, make your opponents hit over you. If they try to hit over you they won't do it consistently. The more you penetrate the less of an angle hitters will have to hit around you. Also, the more you block the ball on your opponent's side of the net, the more likely the ball will come down on their side.

Volleyball Skills for Effective Communication

Teams that have good volleyball passing skills will often try to execute a quick offense. It's important for blockers to communicate their blocking responsibilities before the serve.

Identifying the front row players and setter

As a blocker, you need to know who the possible hitters are. You also need to know if the setter is front row or back row.

A good setter can often draw blockers to them, making the blockers think they need to defend the setter's attack. If you know ahead of time where the setter is on the court (front row or back row) you will know when you need to be prepared to defend a setter attack, and when to ignore the setter and stay with the attackers.

Often a team designates one of the front players as the blocking captain (usually the middle blocker) to facilitate communication.

Call out your opposition

Blockers should develop volleyball skills for identify the opposing setter as front row or back row and also identify the opposing hitters by making calls before the serve.

Examples of call outs by blockers before the serve are...

1. 3 hitters, setter down
2. 2 hitters, setter up
3. 3 hitters, stack right
4. 3 hitters, stack left

Also, you can call out numbers...

1. 3 hitters...stack right...4, 7, and 13
2. setter up...5...2 hitters..4 and 7

Calling out the setter and hitter's is an effective blocking volleyball strategy that will better prepare your team for playing volleyball defense.

Effective communication skills are the volleyball skills that often separate the best teams from everyone else.

VOLLEYBALL TECHNIQUES FOR DIGGING

Teams with volleyball skills for playing great defense often develop great ball control which leads to frustrating their opponents into making hitting errors.

Defensive Positioning

When preparing to dig, keep your feet wide enough apart so you are able to react and move quickly in any direction. Bend your knees and bend at the waist to a

leaning forward position.

Preparing to dig...

1. Feet are wide with the knees bent and out over your toes

2. Shoulders are forward and relaxed

3. Arms are bent and out in front of your body

Digging the Ball

It's best to contact the ball between your knees in front of your body. Ideally, you want to get your hips under the ball so that you have better ball control.

Playing the ball...

1. Anticipate and move to the ball

2. Get your forearms under the ball

3. Lean into the ball as you make contact

4. Dig the ball at the midline of your body if you can

5. If you have to reach outside your body, extend and angle your arms in the direction of the target

Remember to always change your body position to face the hitter.

Hard driven balls are dug often just by getting in good body position. If you are continually able to get into good position for digging (angling your arms to the target every time), you will often dig balls that will stay in play just by them rebounding off of you in the right direction.

Volleyball Skills for Executing Emergency Plays

Learning how to dive

Diving is more popular in the men's volleyball because it takes greater upper body strength to safely execute a dive.

To execute a dive, run towards the ball, push off your back foot and get airborne.

When first learning volleyball skills for diving...

1. Start by standing on a gym mat. At first, just lower yourself down to the mat with your hands.

2. Next, lower down to the ground and then pull

yourself forward with your hands sliding on the ground

3. And finally, bend your knees and get really low to the ground. Extend your body forward, get airborne and slide through on your chest. Practice pulling your body forward with your hands to slide even more.

4. Once you've built confidence, practice by adding a ball.

Most good attackers have developed an array of tough shots to defend. Volleyball skills for keeping the ball off the floor are important to any team's defense.

1. Sprawls

• Forward sprawls

1. Extend your arms underneath the ball and drive the body forward to the floor.

2. If the ball is below knee height, you must adjust your arms so they are parallel to the floor in order to dig the ball. This is done by bend the elbows or curling the wrists. You may also take a step forward and lean to get into a lower position.

• Side sprawls

Sprawl to the side while changing the position of your arms by dropping your inside shoulder. manipulating the position of your arms is important to directing the ball to the target area

2. Dives

Diving consists of staying low to the ground, and gliding through the air to make a play on the ball.

• Keep your shoulders low

As you are about to dive you want to keep your body low to the ground.

- **Keep your body parallel to the floor**

You shouldn't push up off the ground, but push forward. By pushing forward, you will be better at keeping your body parallel to the ground allowing yourself to slide for a better landing.

- **Keep your chin up**

As you are diving, keep your head and chin up.

- **Follow through**

After you play the ball, place your hands on the ground

and pull yourself through by sliding forward.

3. Pancakes

A pancake is most often done when a ball is falling to the floor when the nearest defensive players is far away.

- take a few steps and dive as far as you can through the air.

• slide your hand firmly on the ground.

4. Overhead digs

Learning to play the ball overhead with your fingers when passing the first contact is much different than how you handle the ball for setting attackers. When first learning volleyball skills for overhead digging, practice playing the ball with your hands by keeping your fingers and wrists firm and taut. When digging a hard driven ball, make sure you are initiating contact with the ball. If you let the ball play you, there's a better chance of injuring your fingers.

• Keep your weight on the balls of the feet ready to push the ball forward

• Keep your shoulders behind the ball

• Keep fingers and wrists tensed for better ball control

Player's should be exposed to as many different volleyball skills for playing defensive as possible. There are times when a defensive player can't get in correct position and must react to just keep the ball in play. Therefore, player's should be given the opportunity to develop their own unique techniques and volleyball strategies for digging.

STRATEGIES AND TECHNIQUES FOR PLAYING GOOD DEFENSE

Volleyball tips for making tough plays

Often times during competition players get caught out of position.

Here are a few tips for making defensive plays on balls that are hit deeper than you are ready for and balls tipped

short over the block.

Volleyball Playing Tip for a Short Ball

J-Ball

A j-ball is a term for making a defensive play. The j-

ball technique is usually used on balls that are placed short over the net. Often a run through is done on balls that are tipped short over the net. The player then performs a "J" with the arms to get the ball up.

Face Dig

The face dig is used when players don't have enough time to react and dig with their forearms. All players should practice digging balls hit to their face to avoid the dreaded "six pack".

Pancake

A player may try to pancake a ball that falls in front of them. A pancake is made by a player diving in the air,

extending their body out with the hand sliding on the ground to intercept the ball that is going to hit the floor.

Volleyball Tips for Playing a Deep Ball

Tomahawk

The tomahawk is a method for passing a volleyball overhead. The tomahawk is not for hard driven balls. The

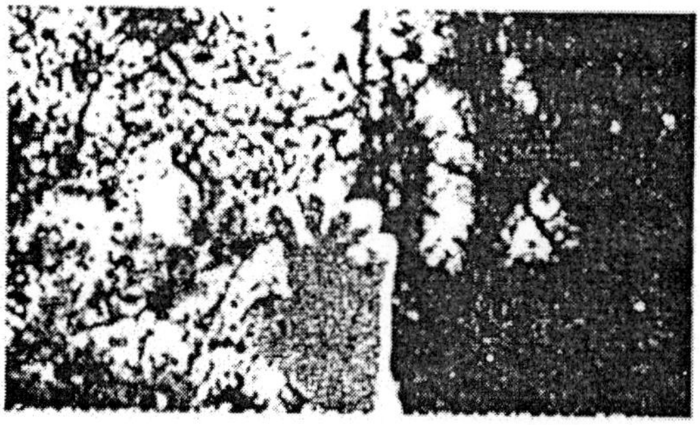

tomahawk is done by putting the hands together, bending the elbows, and making contact with the volleyball overhead.

Camel Poke

The one handed poke can be a real effective way to

Variations

1. Have the hitters swing hard every time so defense can work on digging.

2. Have the hitters tip every time so defense can work on moving to the ball.

3. Have the hitters mix up hits and tips.

Team Pepper, Ball Control — Team Volleyball Drills

This is a variation of the team pepper drill. The goal is to keep the ball in play as long as possible.

This is a great volleyball drill because every player making a play has to really focus on how they play the ball.

For example, every time a hitter hits the ball, they need to focus on hitting the ball in a way that is easiest for their teammates to pass.

Same with tipping. You don't want to disguise the hits and tips because you want the ball to be played in the easiest possible way. This is often very challenging for players that haven't done this before because most players haven't done anything where they have to focus on hitting with control.

Serve the Black Sheep — Team Volleyball Drills

It's good for players to know what it's like for their opponent to serve them every ball, over and over again.

Line up your team in serve receive. Have a server focus on serving to the same player over and over again. The server should be trying to force the same passer to pass every ball in each rotation. The server should be trying to exploit the passer's weaknesses.

For example, if the passer has trouble passing deep serves, work them deep. If the passer likes to take everything with their hands, work them short.

Team volleyball drills such as Black Sheep are great for working on both serving and passing volleyball skills. The server is working on learning how to discover a passer's weaknesses. The passer learns how to concentrate on passing when being picked on.

If they shank a pass, they know another ones coming so they better be ready. Getting served all the time helps the passer develop the mental toughness that's needed for when it's time to step up and make good passes.

Attacking the Setter — Team Volleyball Drills

Setters can often get caught cheating to the net, leaving early to go set in transition. This drill is for training setters to get in the habit of playing defense first.

This volleyball drill needs six players on each side. The coach tosses the ball to the side opposite the setter and the volley is played out.

Every time the hitters hit, they attack so the setter is force to make a defensive play.

For example, if the setter is playing defense in the right back position, the left side hitter attacks the ball down the line or tips the ball over the block so the setter must make a play. Right side players hit hard angle, cut shots, or tips in the setters direction.

This drill is great for the whole team. Hitters can be

creative with their attacks by working on forcing the setter to play volleyball defense first. The setter's teammates are repetitively forced to learn how to adjust the team's offense because of the fact their setter is taking the first ball.

Run Throughs - Team Volleyball Drills

Players are often caught running to make a play on the ball. A run through is a player making a pass while "running through" the ball. This is often done when having to pick up a short shot or tip. A common technique for a run through is the "j-ball".

The j-ball is where the player bends the elbows as they make contact with the ball, to j the ball up. J-balls are a real common technique for when playing short shots or balls close to the floor.

You need a target and player to hand a ball to the coach. All the rest of the players form a line in left back defensive position. The coach stands on a box at the net, directly in front of the players, on the other side of the net.

The drill begins by the coach tipping a ball over the net, and the first player in line runs forward and j's the ball to the target. The player that j'd the ball is now the target. The player that was the target catches the pass and hands the ball to the coach for the next tip. You can also add another player in between the target and coach to help speed up the drill.

There should be a flow to most team volleyball drills. Passer moves to target. Target moves to coach and then after the hand off, the passer moves to the end of the passing line.

This volleyball drill should also be done on the right back side of the court for learning how to j-ball.

The coach can mix up hard hits with tips to help players learn to react and keep them from cheating forward.

Team volleyball drills usually involve the entire team. Therefore, when time is limited, team volleyball drills are an effective way of getting players the "touches on the ball" that is so critical to becoming a good volleyball player.

Team volleyball drills are also important for learning to communicate with teammates. A volleyball team's success is highly dependent on how well teammates communicate with one another.

VOLLEYBALL DRILLS

Volleyball Conditioning, Drills, Skills and Tactics

Volleyball drills are used to enhance various performance factors such as ball control, footwork, and timing on approach jumps or blocks.

Coaches and players need to understand the importance of training with purpose.

A purpose of a drill could be to fix a problem, or improve volleyball skills such as passing or hitting.

Performing your drills with purpose has many benefits...

1. If a player understands the purpose of the drill, rather than just going through the motions, they will be

more interested in the training.

2. Drills for volleyball are important for developing habits. If players are constantly focusing on how to perform a volleyball drill correctly, they will improve their ability to focus during competition.

3. If coaches will set goals and set a specific focus to a drill, they will have better understanding of when to move on or adjust the drill for a better training effect.

Volleyball drills can be broken down into 3 categories...

- Skill and Movement Specific
- Tactical, Systematic, Strategic
- Volleyball Conditioning Specific

Skill and Movement Specific

Volleyball skill and movement drills are the most common types of drills coaches have their players perform.

Skill and movement drills are designed to help players enhance their volleyball skills through repetition.

It's important to note that the purpose of these drills is to develop playing skills such as blocking and setting. These aren't volleyball conditioning drills.

Furthermore, it's important for every player to understand the specific goals of each drill and what skills need to be of focus.

Use repetition to build habits Drills help you develop skills through repetition and practicing with purpose.

Drills for beginning volleyball players should focus on executing the drill with proper technique.

It's important to realize that every second you spend on the court, whether in practice, competition, or just playing a pick up game, you are continually creating or building upon habits.

It's much wiser to develop correct skills early, when you first start playing the game because it's much more difficult to change technique wants habits have been made.

Volleyball drills should be progressive Players need to perform drills progressively, depending on their playing experience and the time of year of training.

Drills range from learning an individual skill such as a forearm pass, to learning combinations of skills such as blocker pulling off the net and then taking an approach to hit.

The difficulty of drills need to progress appropriately with the players in training.

For example, let's say you are performing a drill that involves making a pass then taking an approach to hit. If the focus of the drill is to execute an effective attack hit, and your passing skills are lacking, the focus of the drill will become making better passes.

This drill turns into a passing drill, when the intent was to work on hitting.

Therefore, it is important volleyball drills are modified to fit the ability of the individual players.

Performing these drills with proper focus, repetition, and progression saves time and energy.

Tactical, Systematic, Strategic

Tactical, systematic, and strategic drills focus on team execution.

These drills often involve combinations of playing skills.

Therefore, these drills are often most effective when performed after players have developed their individual playing skills.

Volleyball coaches often have very different philosophies when it comes to playing strategy. Player's have different talents, strengths, and weaknesses that make their teams unique.

For these reasons, strategic drills often vary from one team to another.

It is often wise to run teams through fun drills that are unique and different from what players are used to. Fun volleyball drills will often spark creativity in players and help avoid volleyball player burnout.

Team communication is important Every team needs team drills that help train their players to interact with one another.

Drills that involve players calling the ball to pass or communicating to attackers where to hit are important to success.

Volleyball Conditioning Specific

Volleyball drills can often be designed with the focus being on volleyball conditioning.

If conditioning is one of the goals of a volleyball drill,

coaches need to be aware the energy needed may take away from performing the drill with proper skill technique.

It is most common to perform volleyball conditioning drills in the off-season and pre-season rather than in-season because proper skills execution is less important during these times.

It's usually best to train volleyball skills and conditioning separately when in-season.

Obviously, the volleyball team that has gone through the proper volleyball conditioning in the off-season and pre-season is going to have a much bigger advantage over the teams that haven't.

While the teams that are "out of shape" when the season starts are trying to build up their conditioning, the teams that are in good volleyball condition will just need to work to maintain their high level of conditioning which allows for a much easier time sharpening their skills and working on team tactics and strategies.

VOLLEYBALL STRATEGIES

Skills and Tactics for Improving Performance

Along with enhancing volleyball skills, developing volleyball strategies is an important part to team success.

Serving

Have a philosophy. Whether your philosophy is to serve aggressive or more conservative, you need to have a serving philosophy that will enhance your chances of winning at the level you are competing.

The best servers realize the importance of serving skills. For a moment, the server has complete control of the game. To a degree, their serve dictates how the rally is going to be played out.

I think many coaches don't take serving seriously. Most players serving skills aren't as good as they should be. Serving is a skill that a player has complete control over. Being able to put on a tough serve is a skill players can't afford to not develop.

Learn to serve under pressure. Serving repetitively in practice gives your players a chance to better the skill, but it doesn't give them the experience and pressure of game situations.

Some serving volleyball strategies for learning to serve under pressure

• Find a way to pressure your servers in practice. Play scrimmage in practice and keep score. Penalize a team or individual players for missing serves or for not serving tough enough.

• Keep the pressure on your servers in every match. Every team at some point plays opponents that are under matched. Use this as an opportunity to work on serving.

All too often I see players lose focus and not care how they serve. Even though it may appear you are going to win easily, by using this time to put the pressure on your servers, they'll be ready for when it really counts.

Serving is probably the most under developed skill in volleyball. Every team should develop serving strategies. There's no better way of taking control of a game than with an unstoppable server.

Passing

Passing tough floaters. Common volleyball strategies for passing include having players try and cradle the ball on their arms when they pass, thinking players can get better control of tough floaters the longer the ball stays on their arms.

Although this is usually a good idea, it may be better to be more aggressive when passing, particularly if the ball is floating well.

I like to think of it as, you playing the ball, instead of the ball playing you.

Passing with your hands or forearms? I thing taking the ball with your hands instead of your forearms on

serve receive and other first ball contacts is a good idea in certain situations.

Some good volleyball strategies for using your hands are...

1. Control the ball with your hands, and don't worry about doubling.

2. Seeing as though it's legal to double contact on the first ball, players can be taught to take this first ball with their hands in a more controlled manner by intentionally doubling it for a more control pass.

3. It's usually easier to take hard driven balls (especially deep serves) with your hands than trying to forearm pass them.

The bad thing about using your hands...

• It can sometimes be tough to take a good floater with your hands. Moving sideways to pass a ball with your hands can be pretty difficult.

Also, sometimes you can get caught in deciding between using your hands or forearms to pass. This is a decision that you have just a split-second to make. This is why I think it's a good idea to know before a server even serves whether you have given yourself the option to use your hands or not.

If the server has served balls that were too tough to pass with your hands in the past, it might be a good idea to commit to using your forearms to pass before they even serve.

Serving volleyball strategies for good placement are...

• If you're playing against a passer that is short and

doesn't like using their hands for passing, serve deep.

• If you are playing against a passer that is tall and likes to take everything with their hands, serve short.

Keep your eyes on the ball all the way to your arms. It's tempting to watch the ball with your peripheral vision when passing.

The best volleyball strategies teach passers to follow

the ball all the way onto their arms. Although it takes discipline if you aren't used to it, following the ball all the way does make a difference.

Setting

Setters footwork is important. Many coaches don't care about their setter's footwork and just focus on getting the setter squared and in position to set. I think this is a mistake. Just like any other skill in volleyball, using a consistent technique brings consistent results. Coaches should develop volleyball strategies for better setting involving footwork and ball handling.

By having consistent footwork, (for example, always have your right foot a little further in front of your left

when squaring up) allows for more consistent sets.

Setting volleyball strategies for better accuracy. Also, there is a simple footwork technique that can be applied when a setter is moving from the target position to where the pass is going.

The setter can take a big right step to the spot where the pass is going, pivot on the right foot turning to square up to where they are setting the ball to.

Set tighter or further off simply by adjusting the position of the right foot. If a setter is having trouble keeping their sets off the net, they can simply keep their right foot out in front of them a little bit more than usual.

This will open up their body to the court a little bit which will result in setting further off. On the other hand, if they are having trouble setting too far off, bring that right foot back (by continuing the pivot) closer to a neutral position.

Attacking

Strategies for attacking involve learning many different types of hits and shots. Attackers footwork is often a controversial topic.

Approaching at one speed versus quick last steps. Many volleyball strategies for approaching just emphasize taking fast steps. This may be good for when first teaching volleyball players the approach, but more experienced players need to have a quick last couple steps.

By having your last steps be quicker than your previous steps, you will better utilize the stretch shortening cycle and stretch reflex of your muscles and nervous system therefore increasing your jump and quickness.

Should attackers try to change their steps if they are a wrong-footer? Volleyball strategies for footwork include deciding if it's necessary to correct attackers footwork.

Changing an attackers footwork is probably the hardest skill in volleyball to change.

If you're successful attacking with how your steps are now, it may not be worth the hassle. Obviously, the sooner you start to make the change, the easier it will be.

Making the change really comes down to how

determined a player is. If a player is still fairly inexperienced, it will probably be easier for them to switch the steps because of they have a less developed motor pattern of movement (not as strong of a habit to change).

Advantages of a wrong-footed approach. Right handed hitters that are wrong-footed (also known as goofy-footed) may be better at hitting down the line on the left side.

After stepping right-left-right on the left side, your body is facing more square to the net. Since it's usually easier to hit the direction you're facing, wrong footer's may be more comfortable hitting down the line on their strong side rather than having to turn or cut back angle.

Wrong-footers often have the appearance of jumping really well. Since they're not in the best position to hit after they jump, they spend more time adjusting while in the air.

This extra time they take to adjust their body position makes it appear they jump higher than they actually do. It's really just a greater amount of hang time before they hit.

This is a reason why it's often harder to block wrong-footers, because it's hard to get a read on their body position and the extra time in the air can throw off a blockers timing.

Disadvantages of a wrong-footed approach. I think the biggest disadvantage to being a wrong-footer is the added importance of having to get to the best spot on the court to jump and hit from.

For example, when approaching correctly, a hitter has

the ability to float or drift to the ball if they need to. Their take-off point isn't as important.

So a wrong-footer needs a better read on the ball coming from their setter because it's more critical where they jump to hit from.

Blocking

Most volleyball strategies for blocking can be divided between two concepts, area blocking and read blocking.

Area blocking. Area blocking is when the blockers have predetermine what area they are going to take away from the hitters.

Blocking strategy usually consists of taking away the oppositions most likely shot (area they are most likely going to hit to) with the defense covering the other area of the court.

Read blocking. Teams with bigger blockers and not so great defensive players may use the strategy of read blocking.

With this strategy, blockers are allowed to try and read the hitters during the attack. Blocking decisions are made on the fly and where a blocker is going to block

can be unpredictable.

Obviously this is good that your opponents don't know what you're blocking, but a lot of times neither do your defenders.

Ready position for blocking. Blocking volleyball strategies should include more than just standing at the net with your hands in the air.

Blockers should be in an athletic stance ready to move. They don't just need to be ready to block.

Blockers need to be ready to...

1. Hit an overpass
2. Pull off and pass an overpass
3. Move to block the setter's attack hit or dump
4. Pull off the net and be ready to be set in transition

Digging

Good volleyball strategies for digging include expecting the ball, reading the hitter, and focusing on playing the ball to your target.

Expect the ball to be hit to you. By expecting the ball

to be hit your way, you will be ready to play every ball.

Digging often takes more concentration than passing. You have less time to react and the ball is coming faster. Good volleyball strategies involve anticipating that you will be the one playing the ball to allow better focus on making a successful play.

Read the hitter, but don't cheat. Watch the hitter for clues of what they are going to do with the ball; swing hard, hit a cut shot, tip, etc. You don't need to guess.

With practice you will be able to run down their shots without cheating.

Don't just play the ball; pass it to your target. We often get in awkward positions when making defensive plays. It's easy to get in the habit of just trying to get the ball up.

Really focus on passing to the spot that would be best for that particular play.

Play the ball with two arms if possible. Sometimes you get caught in awkward positions trying to make a defensive play.

Even though it's good to try and make a one arm dig if you have to, the best volleyball strategies involve getting two arms on the ball if possible.

VOLLEYBALL CONDITIONING

Right Volleyball Training and Exercises for Volleyball

Although most coaches are mainly focused on player skills when coaching, volleyball conditioning should be part of every player's preparation strategy.

Are You in Shape for Volleyball?

Conditioning is an important aspect of preparation because volleyball consists of many athletic plays and skills that are physically demanding.

Workout to Get in Volleyball Shape

Volleyball Conditioning Done Right

It continues to amaze me to see volleyball coaches still using outdated conditioning methods that have long been proven useless and ineffective.

How is thirty minutes of low intensity jogging going to prepare you for the 5 to 15 seconds of high intense action that occur in volleyball? It isn't.

Often the biggest mistake coaches make is not training the correct energy systems.

If exercising at a low intensity for a long period of time isn't the answer, then what is?

To answer that question let's briefly look at what occurs in a volleyball match.

In high school volleyball, a match usually consists of match play, best of 3, with all games played to 25 points. Some states are playing best of 5 matches.

To be successful in volleyball, you need to be able to perform quick explosive movements such as short sprints, quick lunges to the side, quick approaches to jump and hit, and jumps to block. Rally's last, on average, for 6 seconds.

A players intensity of effort should be much greater during the rally than between rally's. The time between rally's is when the player recovers. This is the difference between using your body's anaerobic energy systems and aerobic energy systems.

Playing schedule should influence volleyball conditioning

Obviously, a volleyball team's scheduling and playing format varies from state to state. For example, a high school volleyball team may have one match on Tuesday, another on Thursday, and a volleyball tournament on Saturday.

A high school volleyball team in another state could play tris or quads instead of matches. This is where 3 or 4 schools meet and play 2 or 3 matches all on the same night. You will have to build the right type of anaerobic endurance to play optimally for 3 matches instead of only one.

For example, if your team plays 3 matches a night, your volleyball conditioning should be modified to prepare for this. To compete at a high level for all 3 matches, your conditioning should involve more power endurance training.

Collegiate volleyball matches are usually best of 5, with games to 30 points, 5th game to 15.

With college matches being longer, always guaranteed of at least 3 games to 30 points, the college volleyball player needs a higher level of power endurance than the high school volleyball player.

Aerobic vs Anaerobic

Aerobics isn't going to train you for volleyball...

Running Long Distances

Probably the biggest mistake volleyball coaches make

when conditioning their players. A complete waste of time. Running could be used as a part of recovery from intense volleyball workouts, but it really isn't appropriate for volleyball players.

Exercise Machines

Using machines such as treadmills, ellipticals, and stair climbers aren't the best method for your volleyball conditioning. Machines aren't functional for the volleyball player, that is, when using a machine you aren't using your body the way you would on the volleyball court or in real life.

Biking

You aren't going to be a better volleyball player from biking. Your muscles are used in a completely different way on a bike than they are when playing volleyball. A good rule to have for volleyball conditioning is to keep your training "ground based". Your conditioning should take place with your feet in contact with the ground because the majority of movements in volleyball take place in this position.

Anaerobic exercises that should be considered for your volleyball conditioning...

- **Weight Training**

Free weights and medicine balls are common tools for weight training for volleyball to increase strength and power. It's important to understand that free weights are a form of anaerobic training. Volleyball weight training should mainly consist of performing exercises with low repetitions at high intensities with rest periods between sets.

• **Jump Training**

A big part of volleyball is the volleyball approach and the volleyball block. It only makes since to train your body to jump higher, faster, and more explosively.

Speed Training

While long slow running is completely worthless, sprinting is effective for getting volleyball players into shape. Common types of sprinting are court suicides, hill sprints, and sprints up stairs. Developing speed through volleyball conditioning is often combined with plyometric and agility movements.

In order to excel, an athlete should bring an entire strategy to their training that includes volleyball specific conditioning.

Conditioning plays a vital role in a player's ability to develop and enhance various skills.

Highly skilled attacker's have good timing on their approaches when hitting. They also are able to hit the ball in the right direction at the right height and speed. They often have the ability to place the ball where they want to in their opponent's court.

The best blocker's are skilled at doing combinations of lateral movements and jumps to get in position to block.

Setter's need to react to their teammate's passes and get in correct position to set their hitter's. The most athletic setter's often make it look easy.

Libero's and other defensive player's need to dig their opponent's hard swings and pick up cut shots and tips. The best libero's react and move proficiently in the correct direction to make plays on the ball.

These are the skills that player's work on during practice and in scrimmages.

Often the difference between winning and losing is an athlete's level of sport-specific training. Assessing physical talents and abilities is important in designing successful volleyball conditioning programs.

The main factors that influence the design of sport-specific conditioning programs are

- strength
- power
- speed
- agility
- mobility
- flexibility
- coordination
- quickness
- local muscular endurance
- aerobic capacity

Flexibility aids in the development of conditioning and coordination. Both static flexibility and dynamic flexibility are important for volleyball training. An athlete with flexibility generates acceleration over a greater range of motion, thereby increasing speed.

A volleyball player's quality of movement is affected by flexibility. Flexibility training for volleyball should be applied with purpose. When a player has command of their flexibility, they are able to play their sport more strongly, quickly, and expressively.

It is also appropriate to do energy system development for volleyball conditioning to train volleyball specific endurance. The method of training must equal the physical demands specific to volleyball.

The key objectives of volleyball conditioning are to develop strength and explosive power along with agility.

3

FAMOUS VOLLEYBALL PLAYERS

POPULAR BEACH VOLLEYBALL PLAYERS AND INDOOR GREATS

Karch Kiraly

Karch Kiraly is arguably the greatest volleyball player in history of the sport.

Karch Kiraly has the most professional career beach volleyball tournament victories (148).

Karch Kiraly is the only volleyball player to win three gold medals (1984, 1988, 1996).

Karch Kiraly is known as the sparkplug that inspired the 1984 and 1988 USA Men's Olympic Volleyball Teams by playing outstanding volleyball and encouraging his teammates to play their best.

Wearing his hot pink hat, Karch Kiraly was an easily recognizable figure during his days playing volleyball on the beach.

Logan Tom

Logan Tom is a phenomenal athlete and one of the most dynamic volleyball players in the world. Logan Tom's impressive talent has made her one of the most famous volleyball players in the world today.

At 6 feet 1 inch tall, Logan Tom plays volleyball with strength, power, and grace.

Logan Tom was a four-time first-team All-American at Stanford.

Logan Tom was a two-time NCAA National Player of the Year.

Tom was MVP of the NCAA Final Four in 2001.

In the Sydney 2000 Olympics, at 19, Logan Tom was the youngest player on the National Team, yet she started for the team and placed fourth.

Logan Tom is an international superstar that has played professionally in Brazil, Italy and Switzerland.

Misty May Treanor

Misty May-Treanor is arguably the best all-around skilled women's beach volleyball player ever to play the sport.

Misty May Treanor is the Current All-Time Wins Leader.

Misty May was voted the AVP Most Valuable Player in 2005, 2006, and 2007.

Misty May is currently the winningest Female Beach Volleyball Player of all time.

Misty May holds the world record for most consecutive beach tournament victories (15).

Misty May holds the world record for consecutive match victories (90).

Misty May Treanor is one of only three players to be named a two-time AVCA National Player of the Year.

Kerri Walsh

Kerri Walsh currently partners with Misty May Treanor as the best women's beach volleyball team in the world and likely the two most famous volleyball players.

Kerri and Misty had an astonishing win streak of 38 matches in their first year on the AVP Tour.

Kerri and Misty had an unbelievable 89 match win streak on the AVP Tour and the international circuit between 2003 and 2004.

Kerri Walsh is a two-time AVP MVP (2003, 2004).

Kerri Walsh has lead the AVP in both blocks and hitting percentage the last two AVP seasons.

Steve Timmons

In the 80's, Steve Timmons wore a wild red flat top that made him the most identifiable indoor volleyball player in the world.

Considered a pioneer of back row hitting, Steve Timmons combined with his outstanding front row attacking skills made him an unstoppable force.

In 1984, Steve Timmons was named MVP of the Olympics by the FIVB after leading USA to a Gold medal.

Paula Weishoff

Paula Weishoff is one of only 4 USA women's volleyball players to compete in 3 different Olympics.

Throughout her career, Paula Weishoff was a dominating blocker and server.

Paula is the only American volleyball player to have played in Olympic Games 12 years apart (silver in 84, bronze in 92).

4

RULES OF VOLLEYBALL

Volleyball originated in the United States in 1895 as a blend of basketball, baseball, tennis, and handball.

Today, volleyball has spread to 211 countries around the world, and is recognized as a truly international, widely played, popular sport.

Volleyball is a sport played by two teams on a playing court divided by a net. There are different versions available for specific circumstances in order to offer the versatility of the game to everyone.

The object of the game is to send the ball over the net in order to ground it on the opponent's court, and to prevent the same effort by the opponent. The team has three hits for returning the ball (in addition to the block contact).

The ball is put in play with a service: hit by the server over the net to the opponents. The rally continues until the ball is grounded on the playing court, goes "out" or a team fails to return it properly.

In Volleyball, the team winning a rally scores a point (Rally Point System). When the receiving team wins a rally, it gains a point and the right to serve, and its players rotate one position clockwise.

PHILOSOPHY OF RULES AND REFEREEING

Introduction

Volleyball is one of the most successful and popular competitive and recreational sports in the world. It is fast, it is exciting and the action is explosive. Yet volleyball comprises several crucial overlapping elements whose complimentary interactions render it

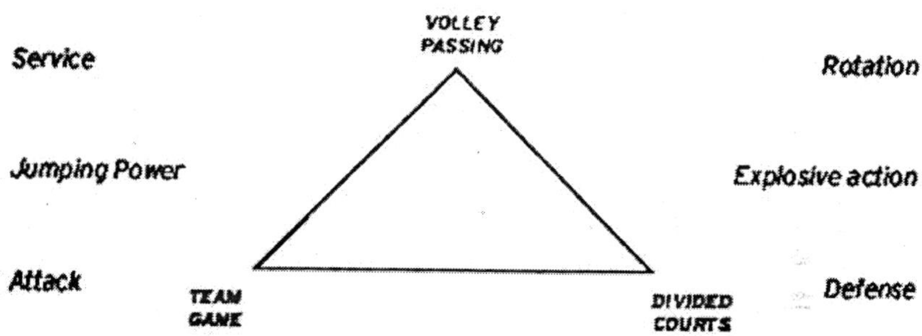

unique amongst rally games:

In recent years the FIVB has made great strides in adapting the game to a modern audience.

This text is aimed at a broad volleyball public - players, coaches, referees, spectators, or commentators for the following reasons:

- understanding the rules allows better play - coaches can create better team structure and tactics, allowing players full rein to display their skills;

- understanding the relationship between rules allows officials to make better decisions.

This introduction at first focuses on volleyball as a competitive sport, before setting out to identify the main qualities required for successful refereeing.

Volleyball is a Competitive Sport

Competition taps latent strengths. It exhibits the best of ability, spirit, creativity and aesthetics. The rules are structured to allow all of these qualities. With a few exceptions, volleyball allows all players to operate both at the net (in attack) and in the back of the court (to defend or serve).

William Morgan, the game's creator, would still recognize it because volleyball has retained certain

distinctive and essential elements over the years. Some of these it shares with other net/ ball/ racquet games:

- service;
- rotation (taking turns to serve);
- attack;
- defence.

Volleyball is, however, unique amongst net games in insisting that the ball is in constant flight – a "flying ball" - and by allowing each team a degree of internal passing before the ball must be returned to the opponents.

The introduction of a specialist defensive player – the Libero – has moved the game forward in terms of rally length and multi-phase play. Modifications to the service rule have changed the act of service from simply a means of putting the ball in play to an offensive weapon.

The concept of rotation is entrenched to allow for all-round athletes. The rules on player positions must permit teams to have flexibility and to create interesting developments in tactics.

Competitors use this framework to contest techniques, tactics and power. The framework also allows players a freedom of expression to enthuse spectators and viewers.

And the image of volleyball is increasingly a good one.

As the game evolves, there is no doubt that it will change – even better, stronger and faster.

The Referee within this Framework

The essence of a good official lies in the concept of fairness and consistency:

- to be fair to every participant

- to be viewed as fair by the spectators.

This demands a huge element of trust – the referee must be trusted to allow the players to entertain:

- by being accurate in his/her judgement

- by understanding why the rule is written

- by being an efficient organiser

- by allowing the competition to flow and by directing it to a conclusion

- by being an educator – using the rules to penalise the unfair or admonish the impolite;

- by promoting the game – that is, by allowing the spectacular elements in the game to shine and the best players to do what they do best: entertain the public Finally we can say that a good referee will use the rules to make the competition a fulfilling experience for all concerned.

To those who have read so far, view the Rules which follow as the current state of development of a great game, but keep in mind why these preceding few paragraphs may be of equal importance to you in your own position within the sport.

THE GAME

FACILITIES AND EQUIPMENT

1. PLAYING AREA

The playing area includes the playing court and the free zone. It shall be rectangular and symmetrical.

Dimensions

The playing court is a rectangle measuring 18 × 9 m, surrounded by a free zone which is a minimum of 3 m wide on all sides.

The free playing space is the space above the playing area which is free from any obstructions. The free playing space shall measure a minimum of 7 m in height from the playing surface.

For FIVB World and Official Competitions, the free zone shall measure a minimum of 5 m from the sidelines and 8 m from the end lines. The free playing space shall measure a minimum of 12.5 m in height from the playing surface.

Playing Surface

1. The surface must be flat, horizontal and uniform. It must not present any danger of injury to the players. It is forbidden to play on rough or slippery surfaces.

For FIVB World and Official Competitions, only a wooden or synthetic surface is allowed. Any surface must be previously approved by the FIVB.

2. On indoor courts the surface of the playing court must be of a light colour.

For FIVB World and Official Competitions, white

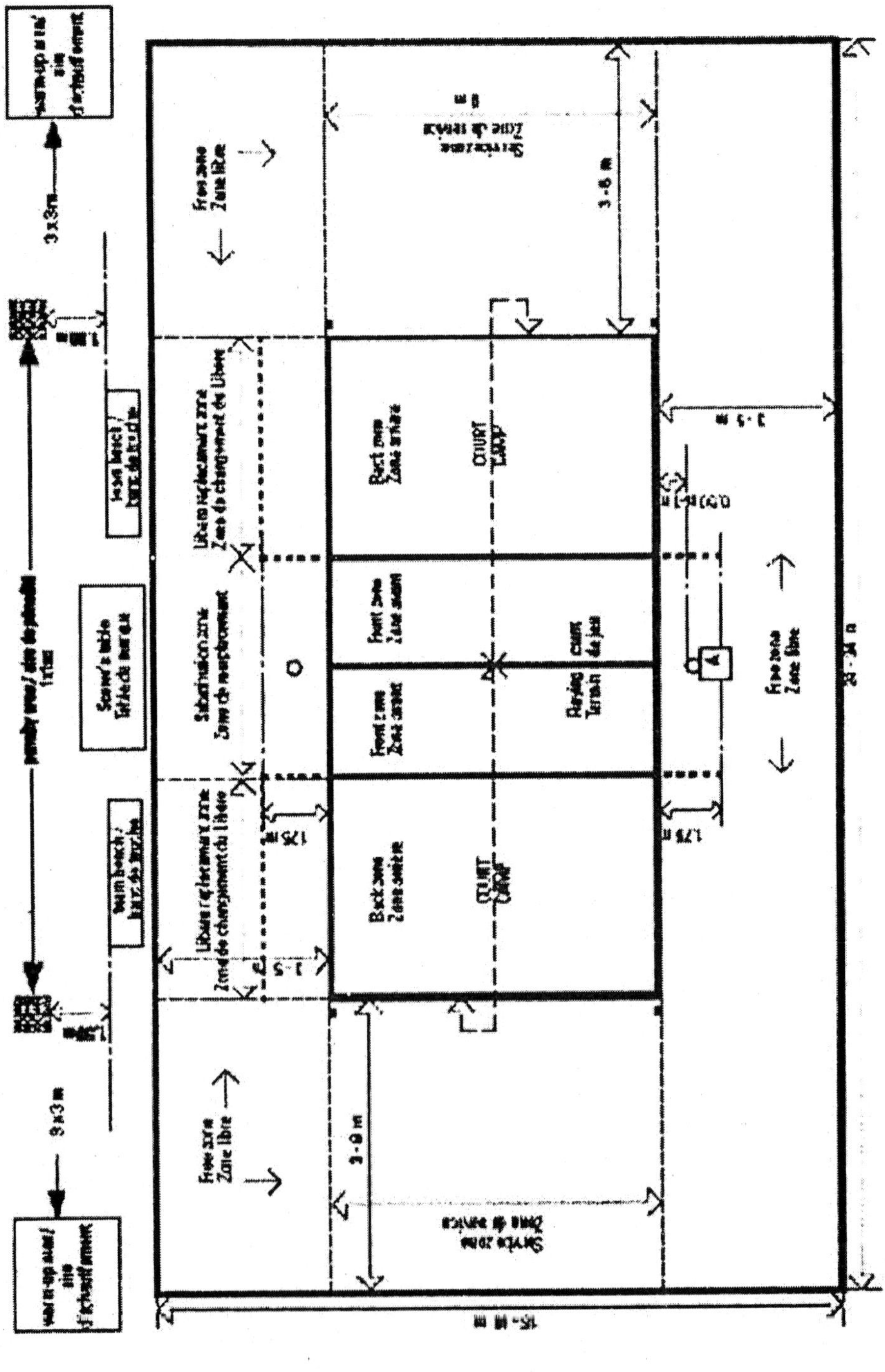
Free zone
Zone libre
Service zone
Zone de service
3 x 3 m
Front zone
Zone avant
Back zone
Zone arrière
Scorer's table
Table de marque
Substitution zone
Zone de remplacement
Libero replacement zone
Zone de changement du Libero
Playing court
Terrain de jeu

colours are required for the lines. Other colours, different from each other, are required for the playing court and the free zone.

3. On outdoor courts a slope of 5 mm per metre is allowed for drainage.

Court lines made of solid materials are forbidden.

LINES ON THE COURT

1. All lines are 5 cm wide. They must be of a light colour which is different from the colour of the floor and from any other lines.

2. Boundary Lines: Two sidelines and two end lines mark the playing court. Both sidelines and end lines are drawn inside the dimensions of the playing court.

3. Centre line: The axis of the centre line divides the playing court into two equal courts measuring 9 × 9 m each; however the entire width of the line is considered to belong to both courts equally. This line extends beneath the net from sideline to sideline.

4. Attack line : On each court, an attack line, whose rear edge is drawn 3 m back from the axis of the centre line, marks the front zone.

For FIVB World and Official Competitions, the attack line is extended by the addition of broken lines from the sidelines, with five 15 cm short lines 5 cm wide, drawn 20 cm from each other to a total length of 1.75 m. The "coach's restriction line" (a broken line which extends from the attack line to the end line of the court, parallel to the side line and 1.75 metres from it) is composed of 15 cm short lines drawn 20 cm apart to mark the limit of the coach's area of operation.

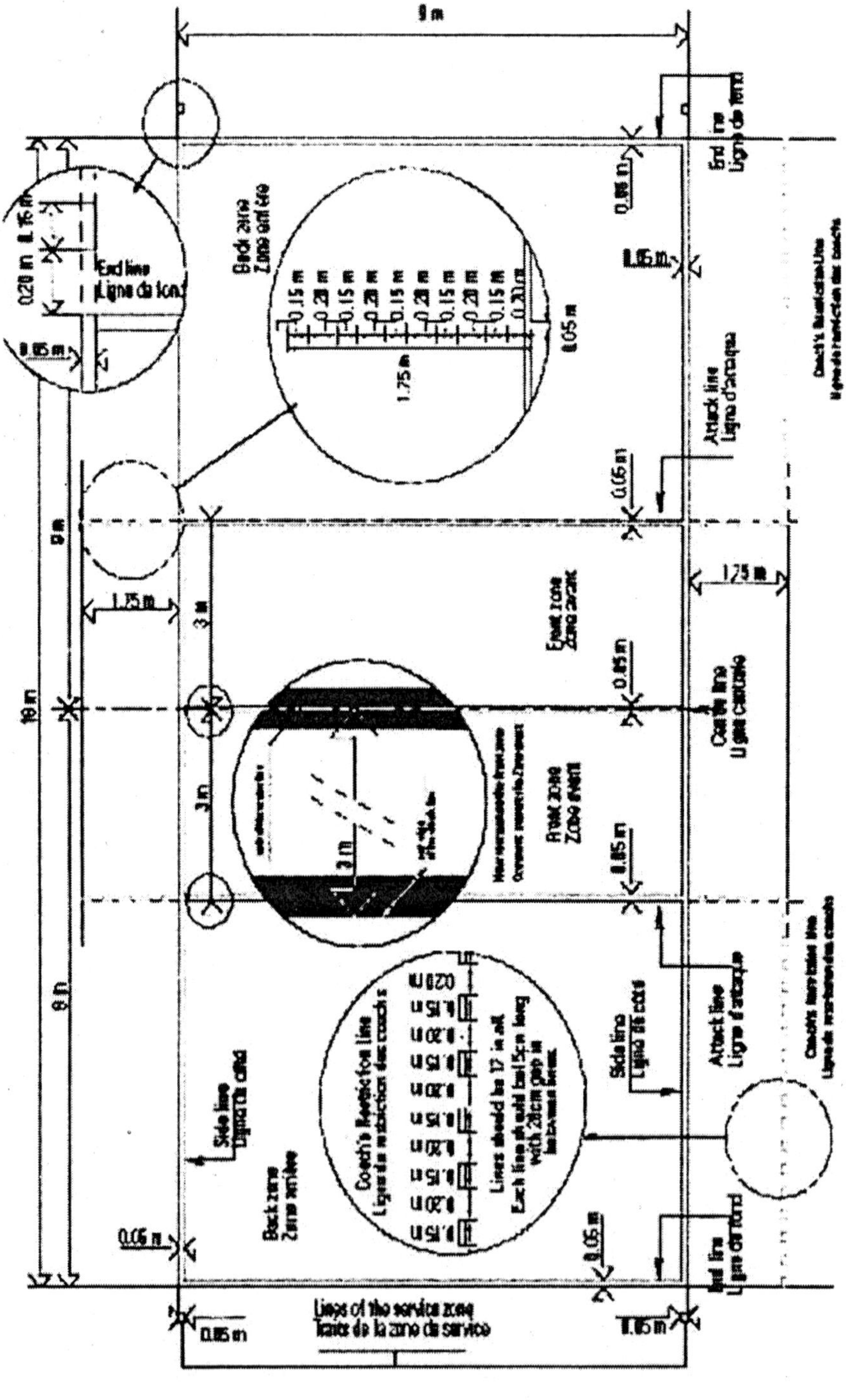
9 m
18 m
End line
Ligne de fond
Attack line
Ligne d'attaque
Centre line
Ligne centrale
Side line
Ligne de côté
Front zone
Zone avant
Back zone
Zone arrière
Coach's Restriction line
Lines of the service zone
Traits de la zone de service

ZONES AND AREAS

1. Front zone: On each court the front zone is limited by the axis of the centre line and the rear edge of the attack line.

The front zone is considered to extend beyond the sidelines to the end of the free zone.

2. Service zone: The service zone is a 9 m wide area behind each end line. It is laterally limited by two short lines, each 15 cm long, drawn 20 cm behind the end line as an extension of the sidelines. Both short lines are included in the width of the service zone.

In depth, the service zone extends to the end of the free zone.

3. Substitution zone: The substitution zone is limited by the extension of both attack lines up to the scorer's table.

4. Libero Replacement Zone: The Libero Replacement Zone is part of the free zone on the side of the team benches, limited by the extension of the attack line up to the end line

5. Warm-up area: For FIVB World and Official Competitions, the warm-up areas, sized approximately 3 x 3 m, are located in both of the bench-side corners, outside the free zone.

6. Penalty area: A penalty area, sized approximately 1 ×1 m and equipped with two chairs, is located in the control area, outside the prolongation of each end line. They may be limited by a 5 cm wide red line.

TEMPERATURE

The minimum temperature shall not be below 10° C (50° F). For FIVB World and Official Competitions, the maximum temperature shall not be higher than 25° C (77° F) and the minimum not lower than 16° C (61° F).

LIGHTING

For FIVB World and Official Competitions, the lighting on the playing area should be 1000 to 1500 lux measured at 1 m above the surface of the playing area.

2. NET AND POSTS

Height of the Net

1. Placed vertically over the centre line there is a net whose top is set at the height of 2.43 m for men and 2.24 m for women.

2. Its height is measured from the centre of the playing court. The net height (over the two sidelines) must be exactly the same and must not exceed the official height by more than 2 cm.

STRUCTURE

The net is 1 m wide and 9.50 to 10 metres long (with 25 to 50 cm on each side of the side bands), made of 10 cm square black mesh.

At its top a horizontal band, 7 cm wide, made of two-fold white canvas, is sewn along its full length. Each extreme end of the band has a hole, through which passes a cord, fastening the band to the posts for keeping its top taut.

Within the band, a flexible cable fastens the net to the posts and keeps its top taut.

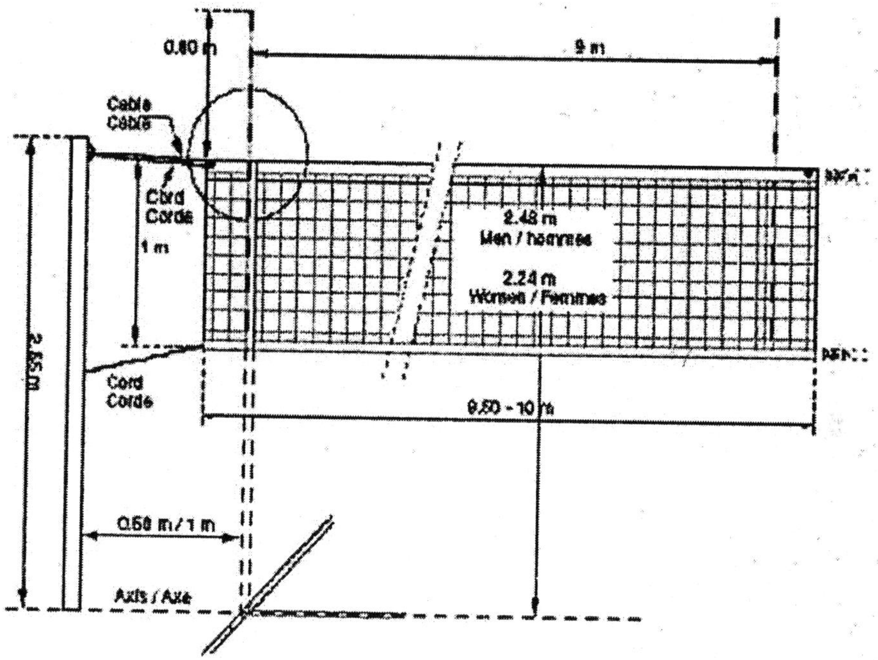
0.80 m
9 m
Cable
Cable
Cord
Corde
1 m
2.55 m
2.43 m
Men / hommes
2.24 m
Women / Femmes
Cord
Corde
9.50 - 10 m
0.50 m / 1 m
Axis / Axe

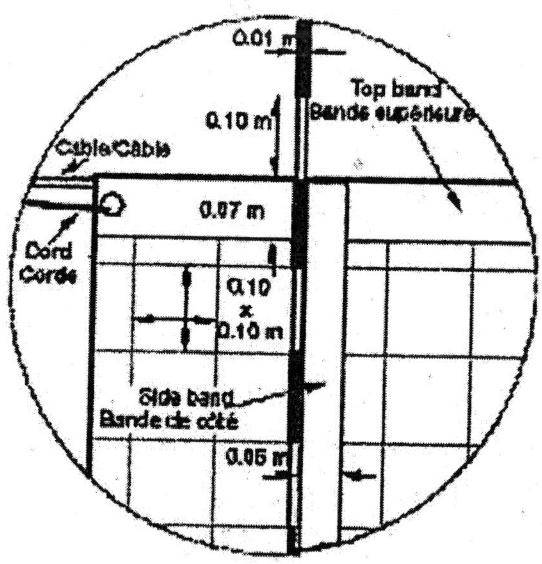
0.01 m
Top band
Bande supérieure
0.10 m
Cable/Câble
0.07 m
Cord
Corde
0.10
x
0.10 m
Side band
Bande de côté
0.05 m

At the bottom of the net there is another horizontal band, 5cm wide, similar to the top band, through which is threaded a rope. This rope fastens the net to the posts and keeps its lower part taut.

SIDE BANDS

Two white bands are fastened vertically to the net and placed directly above each sideline.

They are 5 cm wide and 1 m long, and are considered as part of the net.

ANTENNAE

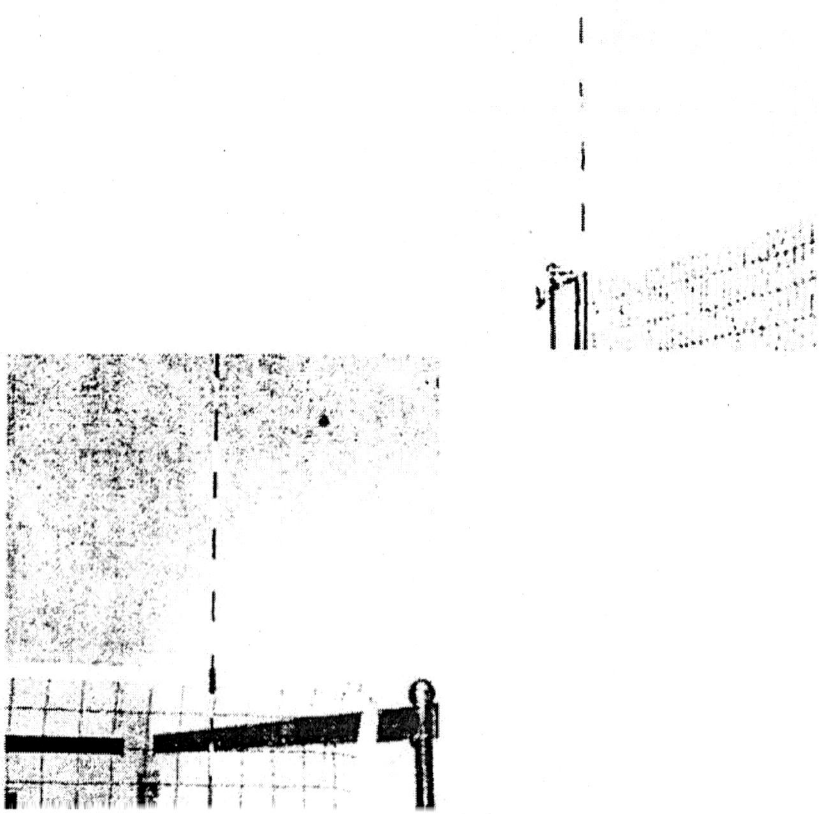

An antenna is a flexible rod, 1.80 m long and 10 mm in diameter, made of fibreglass or similar material.

An antenna is fastened at the outer edge of each side band. The antennae are placed on opposite sides of the net.

The top 80 cm of each antenna extends above the net and is marked with 10 cm stripes of contrasting colour, preferably red and white.

The antennae are considered as part of the net and laterally delimit the crossing space.

POSTS

1. The posts supporting the net are placed at a distance of 0.50 -1.00 m outside the sidelines. They are 2.55 m high and preferably adjustable.

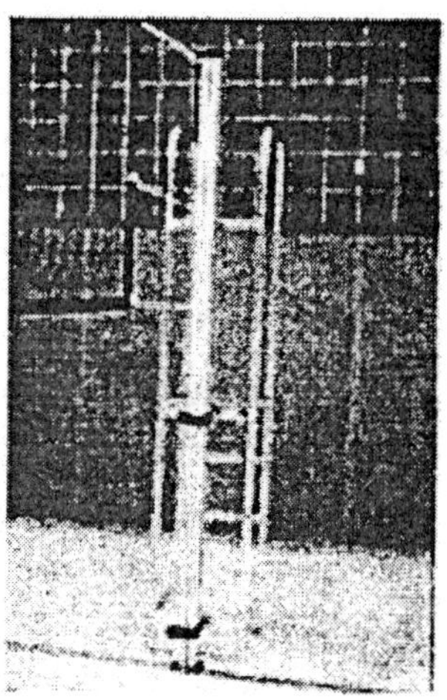

For all FIVB World and Official Competitions, the posts supporting the net are placed at a distance of 1 m outside the sidelines.

2. The posts are rounded and smooth, fixed to the ground without wires. There shall be no dangerous or obstructing devices.

ADDITIONAL EQUIPMENT

All additional equipment is determined by FIVB regulations.

3. BALLS

STANDARDS

The ball shall be spherical, made of a flexible leather or synthetic leather case with a bladder inside made of rubber or a similar material.

Its colour may be a uniform light colour, or a combination of colours. Synthetic leather material and colour combinations of balls used in International Official competitions should comply with FIVB standards.

Its circumference is 65-67 cm and its weight is 260-280 g. Its inside pressure shall be 0.30 to 0. 325 kg/cm2 (4.26 to 4.61 psi) (294.3 to 318.82 mbar or hPa)

UNIFORMITY OF BALLS

All balls used in a match must have the same

standards regarding circumference, weight, pressure, type, colour, etc.

FIVB World and Official Competitions, as well as National or League Championships must be played with FIVB approved balls, unless by agreement of FIVB.

THREE-BALL SYSTEM

For FIVB World and Official Competitions, three balls shall be used. In this case, six ball retrievers are stationed, one at each corner of the free zone and one behind each referee.

PARTICIPANTS

4. TEAMS

TEAM COMPOSITIONS

1. A team may consist of up to 12 players, one coach, one assistant coach, one trainer and one medical doctor.

For FIVB, World and Official Competitions, the medical doctor must be accredited beforehand by the FIVB. For FIVB and World Competitions for Seniors, a team may consist of a maximum of fourteen (14) players (a maximum of twelve (12) regular players.)

2. One of the players, other than the Libero, is the team captain, who shall be indicated on the score sheet.

3. Only the players recorded on the score sheet may enter the court and play in the match. Once the coach and the team captain have signed the score sheet, the recorded players cannot be changed.

LOCATION OF THE TEAM

1. The players not in play should either sit on their team bench or be in their warm-up area. The coach and other team members sit on the bench, but may temporarily leave it.

The benches for the teams are located beside the scorer's table, outside the free zone.

2. Only the team members are permitted to sit on the bench during the match and to participate in the warm-up session.

3. Players not in play may warm-up without balls as follows:

1. during play: in the warm-up areas;

2. during time-outs and technical time-outs: in the free zone behind their court.

3. During set intervals, players may warm-up using balls in the free zone.

EQUIPMENT

A player's equipment consists of a jersey, shorts, socks (the uniform) and sport shoes.

1. The colour and the design for the jerseys, shorts and socks must be uniform for the team (except for the Libero). The uniforms must be clean.

2. The shoes must be light and pliable with non-marking rubber or composite soles without heels.

For FIVB World and Official Competitions, it is forbidden to wear shoes which are predominantly black.

3. Players' jerseys must be numbered from 1 to 18.

For FIVB World and Official Competitions, players' jerseys must be numbered from 1 to 20

1. The number must be placed on the jersey at the centre of the front and of the back. The colour and brightness of the numbers must contrast with the colour and brightness of the jerseys.

2. The number must be a minimum of 15 cm in height on the chest, and a minimum of 20 cm in height on the back. The stripe forming the numbers shall be a minimum of 2 cm in width.

to assume the role of game captain. This game captain maintains his/her responsibilities until he/she is substituted, or the team captain returns to play, or the set ends.

When the ball is out of play, only the game captain is authorized to speak to the referees:

1. to ask for an explanation on the application or interpretation of the Rules, and also to submit the requests or questions of his/her teammates.

If the game captain does not agree with the explanation of the first referee, he/she may choose to protest against such decision and immediately indicates to the first referee that he/she reserves the right to record an official protest on the score sheet at the end of the match;

2. to ask authorization:

(i) to change all or part of the equipment

(ii) to verify the positions of the teams

(iii) to check the floor, the net, the ball, etc.

3. In the absence of the coach: to request time-outs and substitutions.

AT THE END OF THE MATCH, the team captain:

1. thanks the referees and signs the score sheet to ratify the outcome

2. when it has been notified in due time to the first referee, may confirm and record on the score sheet an official protest regarding the referee's application or interpretation of the Rules.

COACH

1 Throughout the match, the coach conducts the play of his/her team from outside the playing court. He/she selects the starting line-ups, their substitutes, and takes time-outs. In these functions his/her contacting official is the second referee.

2. PRIOR TO THE MATCH, the coach records or checks the names and numbers of his/her players on the score sheet, and then signs it.

3. DURING THE MATCH, the coach:

(i) prior to each set, gives the second referee or the scorer the line-up sheet(s) duly filled in and signed;

(ii) sits on the team bench nearest to the scorer, but may leave it;

(iii) requests time-outs and substitutions;

(iv) may, as well as other team members, give instructions to the players on the court. The coach may give these instructions while standing or walking within the free zone in front of his/her team's bench from the extension of the attack line up to the warm-up area, without disturbing or delaying the match.

For FIVB World and Official Competitions, the coach is restricted to performing his/her function behind the coach's restriction line.

ASSISTANT COACH

1. The assistant coach sits on the team bench, but has no right to intervene in the match.

2. Should the coach have to leave his/her team for any reason including sanction, the assistant coach may, at the request of the game captain and with the authorization of the first referee, assume the coach's functions for the duration of the absence.

PLAYING FORMAT

6. TO SCORE A POINT, TO WIN A SET AND THE MATCH

TO SCORE A POINT

1. Point: A team scores a point:

(i) by successfully grounding the ball on the opponent's court.

(ii) when the opponent team commits a fault.

(iii) when the opponent team receives a penalty.

2. Fault :

A team commits a fault by making a playing action contrary to the rules (or by violating them in some other way). The referees judge the faults and determine the consequences according to the Rules:

(i) If two or more faults are committed successively, only the first one is counted.

(ii) If two or more faults are committed by opponents simultaneously, a DOUBLE FAULT is called and the rally is replayed.

3. Rally and completed rally

A rally is the sequence of playing actions from the moment of the service hit by the server until the ball is out of play. A completed rally is the sequence of playing actions which results in the award of a point.

(i) if the serving team wins a rally, it scores a point and continues to serve;

(ii) if the receiving team wins a rally, it scores a point and it must serve next.

TO WIN A SET

A set (except the deciding, 5th set) is won by the team which first scores 25 points with a minimum lead of two points. In the case of a 24-24 tie, play is continued until a two-point lead is achieved (26-24; 27-25; ...).

TO WIN THE MATCH

(i) The match is won by the team that wins three sets.

(ii) In the case of a 2-2 tie, the deciding set (the 5th) is played to 15 points with a minimum lead of 2 points.

DEFAULT AND INCOMPLETE TEAM

(i) If a team refuses to play after being summoned to do so, it is declared in default and forfeits the match with the result 0-3 for the match and 0-25 for each set.

(ii) A team that, without justifiable reason, does not appear on the playing court on time is declared in default with the same result.

(iii) A team that is declared INCOMPLETE for the set or for the match, loses the set or the match. The opponent team is given the points, or the points and the sets, needed to win the set or the match. The incomplete team keeps its points and sets.

7. STRUCTURE OF PLAY

THE TOSS

Before the match, the first referee carries out a toss to decide upon the first service and the sides of the court in the first set.

If a deciding set is to be played, a new toss will be carried out.

(i) The toss is taken in the presence of the two team captains.

(ii) The winner of the toss chooses:

EITHER

(a) the right to serve or to receive the service,

OR

(b) the side of the court.

The loser takes the remaining choice.

(iii) In the case of consecutive warm-ups, the team that has the first service takes the first turn at the net.

WARM-UP SESSION

1. Prior to the match, if the teams have previously had a playing court at their disposal, they are entitled to a 6-minute warm-up period together at the net; if not, they may have 10 minutes

2. If either captain requests separate (consecutive) warm-ups at the net, the teams may do so for 3 minutes each or 5 minutes each.

TEAM STARTING LINE-UP

1. There must always be six players per team in play.

The team's starting line-up indicates the rotational order of the players on the court. This order must be maintained throughout the set.

2. Before the start of each set, the coach has to present the starting lineup of his/her team on a line-up sheet. The sheet is submitted, duly filled in and signed, to the second referee or the scorer.

3. The players who are not in the starting line-up of a set are the substitutes for that set (except for the Libero).

4. Once the line-up sheet has been delivered to the second referee or scorer, no change in line-up may be authorized without a regular substitution.

5. Discrepancies between players' position on court and on the line-up sheet are dealt with as follows:

(i) when such a discrepancy is discovered before the start of the set, players' positions must be rectified according to that on the line-up sheet - there will be no sanction;

(ii) when, before the start of the set, a player on court is found not to be registered on the line-up sheet of that set, this player must be changed to conform to the line-up sheet - there will be no sanction;

(iii) however, if the coach wishes to keep such non-recorded player(s) on the court, he/she has to request regular substitution(s), which will then be recorded on the score sheet.

If a discrepancy between player positions and the line up sheet is discovered later, the team at fault must revert to the correct positions. All points scored by the team from the exact moment of the fault up to the discovery of the fault are cancelled. The opponent's points remain valid and in addition they receive a point and the next service.

POSITIONS

At the moment the ball is hit by the server, each team must be positioned within its own court in the rotational order (except the server).

(i) The positions of the players are numbered as follows:

(a) the three players along the net are front-row players and occupy positions 4 (front-left), 3 (front-centre) and 2 (front-right);1

(b) the other three are back-row players occupying positions 5 (back-left), 6 (back-centre) and 1 (back-right).

(ii) Relative positions between players:

(a) each back-row player must be positioned further

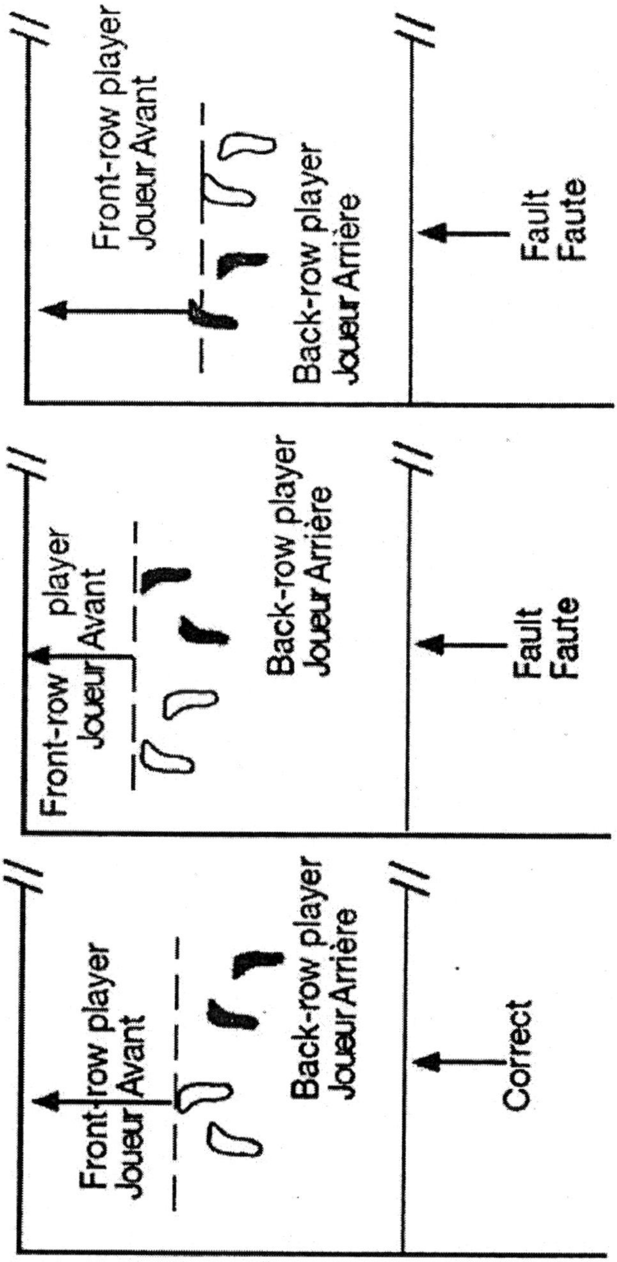

Front-row player
Joueur Avant
Back-row player
Joueur Arrière
Correct
Front-row player
Joueur Avant
Back-row player
Joueur Arrière
Fault
Faute
Front-row player
Joueur Avant
Back-row player
Joueur Arrière
Fault
Faute

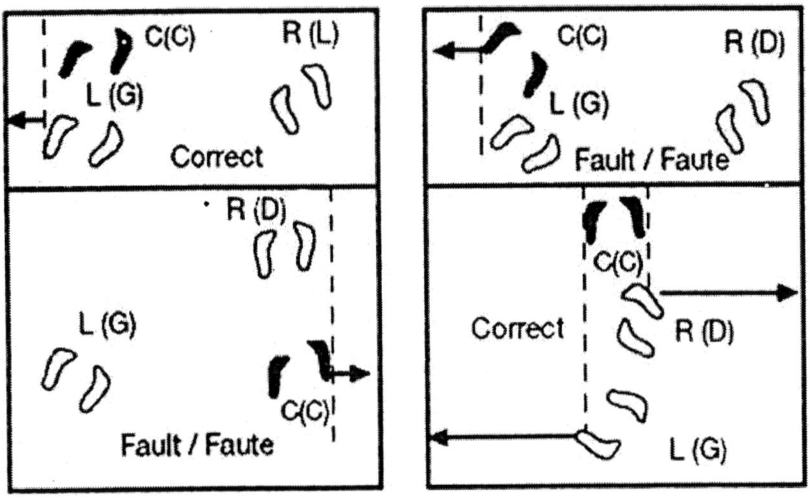

C(C) - Centre player / Joueur centre
R(D) - Right player / Joueur droit
L(G) - Left player / Joueur gauche

back from the centre line than the corresponding front-row player;

(b) the front-row players and the back-row players, respectively, must be positioned laterally in the order.

(iii) The positions of players are determined and controlled according to the positions of their feet contacting the ground as follows:

(i) each front-row player must have at least a part of his/her foot closer to the centre line than the feet of the corresponding back-row player;

(ii) each right (left) side player must have at least a part of his/her foot closer to the right (left) sideline than the feet of the centre player in that row.

(iv) After the service hit, the players may move around and occupy any position on their court, and the free zone.

POSITIONAL FAULT

1. The team commits a positional fault, if any player is not in his/her correct position at the moment the ball is hit by the server.

2. If the server commits a serving fault at the moment of the service hit, the server's fault is counted before a positional fault.

3. If the service becomes faulty after the service hit, it is the positional fault that will be counted.

4. A positional fault leads to the following consequences:

(i) the team is sanctioned with a point and service to the opponent;

(ii) players' positions are rectified.

ROTATION

1. Rotational order is determined by the team's starting line-up, and controlled with the service order, and players' positions, throughout the set.

2. When the receiving team has gained the right to serve, its players rotate one position clock-wise: the player in position 2 rotates to position 1 to serve, the player in position 1 rotates to position 6, etc.

ROTATIONAL FAULT

1. A rotational fault is committed when the SERVICE

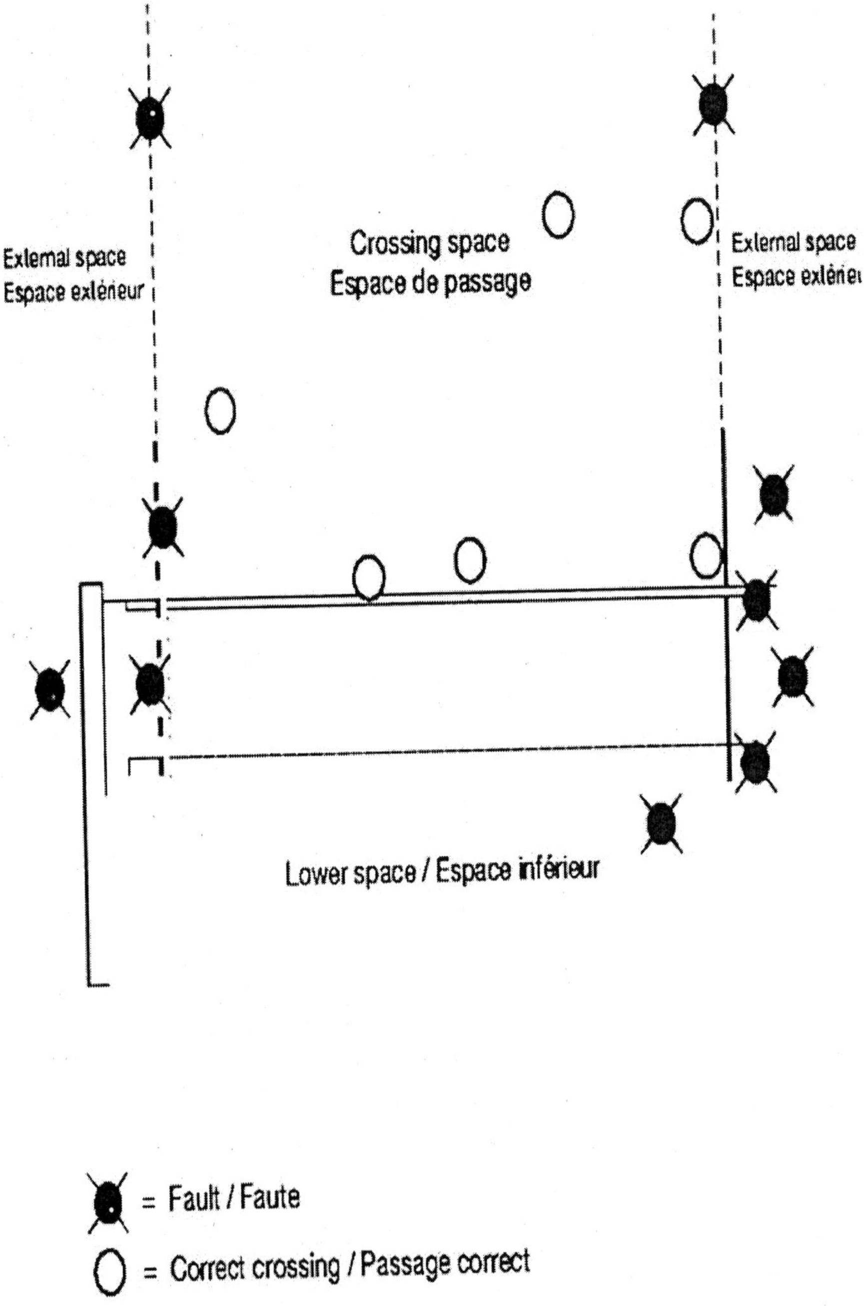
External space
Espace extérieur
Crossing space
Espace de passage
External space
Espace extérieu
Lower space / Espace inférieur
= Fault / Faute
= Correct crossing / Passage correct

is not made according to the rotational order. It leads to the following consequences:

(i) the team is sanctioned with a point and service to the opponent;

(ii) the players' rotational order is rectified. 7.6.1

2. Additionally, the scorer should determine the exact moment when the fault was committed and all points scored subsequently by the team at fault must be cancelled. The opponent's points remain valid.

If that moment cannot be determined, no point(s) cancellation takes place, and a point and service to the opponent is the only sanction.

PLAYING ACTIONS

8. STATES OF PLAY

BALL IN PLAY

The ball is in play from the moment of the hit of the service authorized by the first referee.

BALL OUT OF PLAY

The ball is out of play at the moment of the fault which is whistled by one of the referees; in the absence of a fault, at the moment of the whistle.

BALL "IN"

The ball is "in" when it touches the floor of the playing court including the boundary lines.

BALL "OUT"

The ball is "out" when:

1. the part of the ball which contacts the floor is completely outside the boundary lines;

2. it touches an object outside the court, the ceiling or a person out of play;

3. it touches the antennae, ropes, posts or the net itself outside the side bands;

4. it crosses the vertical plane of the net either partially or totally outside the crossing space.

5. it crosses completely the lower space under the net.

9. PLAYING THE BALL

Each team must play within its own playing area and space. The ball may, however, be retrieved from beyond the free zone.

TEAM HITS

A hit is any contact with the ball by a player in play.

The team is entitled to a maximum of three hits, for returning the ball. If more are used, the team commits the fault of: "FOUR HITS".

CONSECUTIVE CONTACTS

A player may not hit the ball two times consecutively.

SIMULTANEOUS CONTACTS

Two or three players may touch the ball at the same moment.

(i) When two (three) team-mates touch the ball simultaneously, it is counted as two (three) hits (with the exception of blocking). If they reach for the ball, but only one of them touches it, one hit is counted.

A collision of players does not constitute a fault.

(ii) When two opponents touch the ball simultaneously over the net and the ball remains in play, the team receiving the ball is entitled to another three hits. If such a ball goes "out", it is the fault of the team on the opposite side.

(iii) If simultaneous hits by two opponents over the net lead to extended contact with the ball, play continues.

ASSISTED HIT

Within the playing area, a player is not permitted to take support from a team-mate or any structure/object in order to hit the ball.

However, a player who is about to commit a fault (touch the net or cross the centre line, etc.) may be stopped or held back by a teammate.

CHARACTERISTICS OF THE HIT

1. The ball may touch any part of the body.

2. The ball must not be caught and/or thrown. It can rebound in any direction.

3. The ball may touch various parts of the body, provided that the contacts take place simultaneously.

Exceptions:

1. at blocking, consecutive contacts may be made by one or more blocker(s) provided that the contacts occur during one action.

2. at the first hit of the team, the ball may contact various parts of the body consecutively provided that the contacts occur during one action.

FAULTS IN PLAYING THE BALL

1. FOUR HITS: a team hits the ball four times before returning it.

2. ASSISTED HIT: a player takes support from a teammate or any structure/object in order to hit the ball within the playing area.

3. CATCH: the ball is caught and/or thrown; it does not rebound from the hit.

4. DOUBLE CONTACT: a player hits the ball twice in succession or the ball contacts various parts of his/her body in succession.

10. BALL AT THE NET

BALL CROSSING THE NET

1. The ball sent to the opponent's court must go over the net within the crossing space. The crossing space is the part of the vertical plane of the net limited as follows:

(i) below, by the top of the net;

(ii) at the sides, by the antennae, and their imaginary extension;

2. The ball that has crossed the net plane to the opponent's free zone totally or partly through the external space, may be played back within the team hits, provided that:

(i) the opponent's court is not touched by the player;

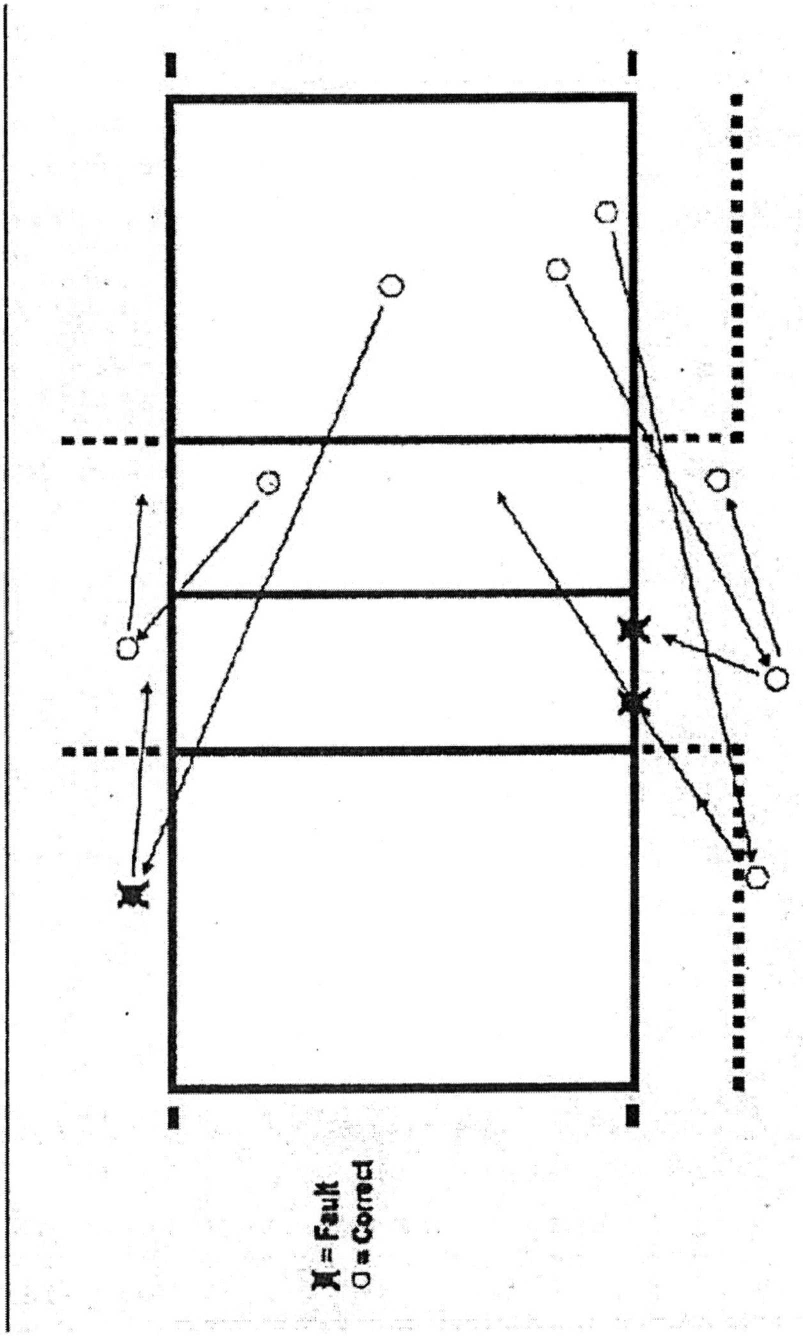
= Fault
= Correct

(ii) the ball, when played back, crosses the net plane again totally or partly through the external space on the same side of the court. The opponent team may not prevent such action.

3. The ball that is heading towards the opponent's court through the lower space is in play until the moment it has completely crossed the vertical plane of the net.

BALL TOUCHING THE NET

While crossing the net, the ball may touch it.

BALL IN THE NET

1. A ball driven into the net may be recovered within the limits of the three team hits.

2. If the ball rips the mesh of the net or tears it down, the rally is cancelled and replayed.

11. PLAYER AT THE NET

REACHING BEYOND THE NET

1. In blocking, a blocker may touch the ball beyond the net, provided that he/she does not interfere with the opponent's play before or during the latter's attack hit.

2. After an attack hit, a player is permitted to pass his/her hand beyond the net, provided that the contact has been made within his/her own playing space.

PENETRATION UNDER THE NET

1. It is permitted to penetrate into the opponent's space under the net, provided that this does not interfere with the opponent's play.

2. Penetration into the opponent's court, beyond the centre line:

(i) to touch the opponent's court with a foot (feet) is permitted, provided that some part of the penetrating foot (feet) remains either in contact, with or directly above the centre line.

(ii) to touch the opponent's court with any part of the body above the feet is permitted provided that it does not interfere with the opponent's play.

(iii) A player may enter the opponent's court after the ball goes out of play.

(iv) Players may penetrate into the opponent's free one provided that they do not interfere with the OPPONENT'S play.

CONTACT WITH THE NET

1. Contact with the net by a player is not a fault, unless it interferes with the play.

2. Players may touch the post, ropes, or any other object outside the antennae, including tne net itself, provided that it does not interfere with play.

3. When the ball is driven into the net, causing it to touch an opponent, no fault is committed.

PLAYER'S FAULTS AT THE NET

1. A player touches the ball or an opponent in the opponent's space before or during the opponent's attack hit.

2. A player interferes with the opponent's play while penetrating into the opponent's space under the net.

3. A player's foot (feet) penetrates completely into the opponent's court.

4. A player interferes with the opponent's play by (amongst others):

- touching the top band of the net or the top 80 cm of the antenna during his/her action of playing the ball, or

- taking support from the net simultaneously with playing the ball, or

- creating an advantage over the opponent, or

- making actions which hinder an opponent's legitimate attempt to play the ball

12. SERVICE

The service is the act of putting the ball into play, by

the back right player, placed in the service zone.

FIRST SERVICE IN A SET

1. The first service of the first set, as well as that of the deciding set (the 5th) is executed by the team determined by the toss.

2. The other sets will be started with the service of the team that did not serve first in the previous set.

SERVICE ORDER

1. The players must follow the service order recorded on the line-up sheet.

(i) After the first service in a set, the player to serve is determined as follows:

(a) when the serving team wins the rally, the player (or his/her substitute) who served before, serves again;

(b) when the receiving team wins the rally, it gains the right to serve and rotates before actually serving. The player who moves from the front right position to the back-right position will serve.

AUTHORIZATION OF THE SERVICE

The first referee authorizes the service, after having checked that the two teams are ready to play and that the server is in possession of the ball.

EXECUTION OF THE SERVICE

1. The ball shall be hit with one hand or any part of the arm after being tossed or released from the hand(s).

2. Only one toss or release of the ball is allowed. Dribbling or moving the ball in the hands is permitted.

3. At the moment of the service hit or take-off for a jump service, the server must not touch the court (the end line included) or the floor outside the service zone.

After the hit, he/she may step or land outside the service zone, or inside the court.

4. The server must hit the ball within 8 seconds after the first referee whistles for service.

5. A service executed before the referee's whistle is cancelled and repeated.

SCREENING

1. The players of the serving team must not prevent their opponent, through individual or collective screening, from seeing the server or the flight path of the ball.

2. A player, or group of players, of the serving team makes a screen by waving arms, jumping or moving sideways, during the execution of the service, or by standing grouped to hide the flight path of the ball.

FAULTS MADE DURING THE SERVICE

1. Serving faults

The following faults lead to a change of service even if the opponent is out of position. The server:

(i) violates the service order,

(ii) does not execute the service properly.

2. Faults after the service hit.

After the ball has been correctly hit, the service becomes a fault (unless a player is out of position) if the

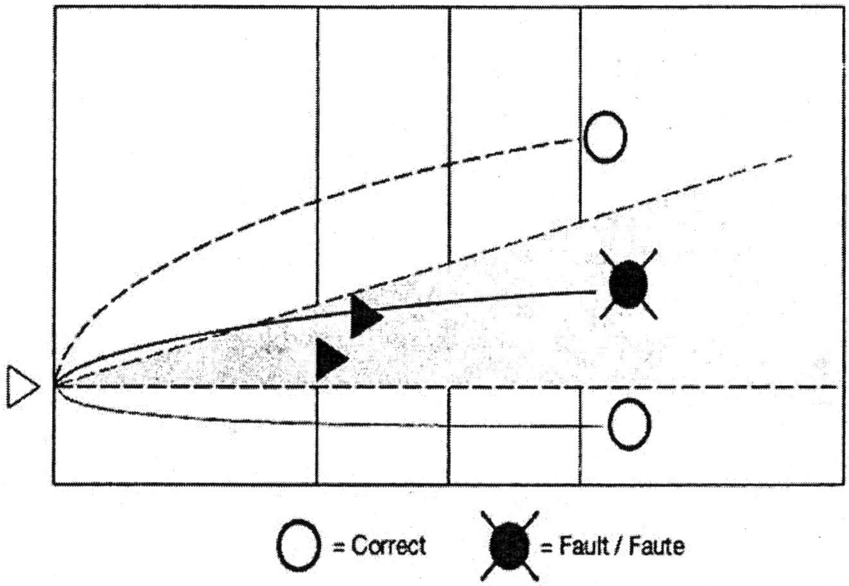

ball:

(i) touches a player of the serving team or fails to cross the vertical plane of the net completely through the crossing space;

(ii) goes "out"; 8.4,

(iii) passes over a screen.

SERVING FAULTS AND POSITIONAL FAULTS

(i) If the server makes a fault at the moment of the service hit (improper execution, wrong rotational order, etc.) and the opponent is out of position, it is the serving fault which is sanctioned.

(ii) Instead, if the execution of the service has been correct, but the service subsequently becomes faulty (goes out, goes over a screen, etc.), the positional fault has taken place first and is sanctioned.

13. ATTACK HIT

CHARACTERISTICS OF THE ATTACK HIT

(1) All actions which direct the ball towards the opponent, with the exception of service and block, are considered as attack hits.

(2) During an attack hit, tipping is permitted only if the ball is cleanly hit, and not caught or thrown.

(3) An attack hit is completed at the moment the ball completely crosses the vertical plane of the net or is touched by an opponent.

RESTRICTIONS OF THE ATTACK HIT

(1) A front-row player may complete an attack hit at any height, provided that the contact with the ball has been made within the player's own playing space.

(2) A back-row player may complete an attack hit at any height from behind the front zone:

(i) at his/her take-off, the player's foot (feet) must neither have touched nor crossed over the attack line;

(ii) after his/her hit, the player may land within the front zone.

(3) A back-row player may also complete an attack hit from the front zone, if at the moment of the contact part of the ball is lower than the top of the net.

(4) No player is permitted to complete an attack hit on the OPPONENT'S service, when the ball is in the front zone and entirely higher than the top of the net.

FAULTS OF THE ATTACK HIT

1 A player hits the ball within the playing space of

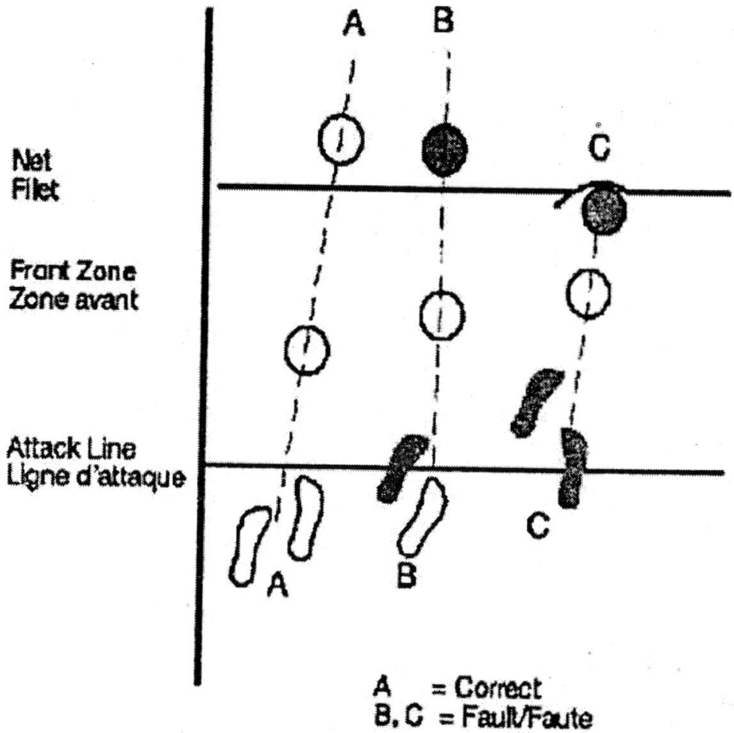
A
B
Net
Filet
C
Front Zone
Zone avant
Attack Line
Ligne d'attaque
A
B
C
A = Correct
B, C = Fault/Faute

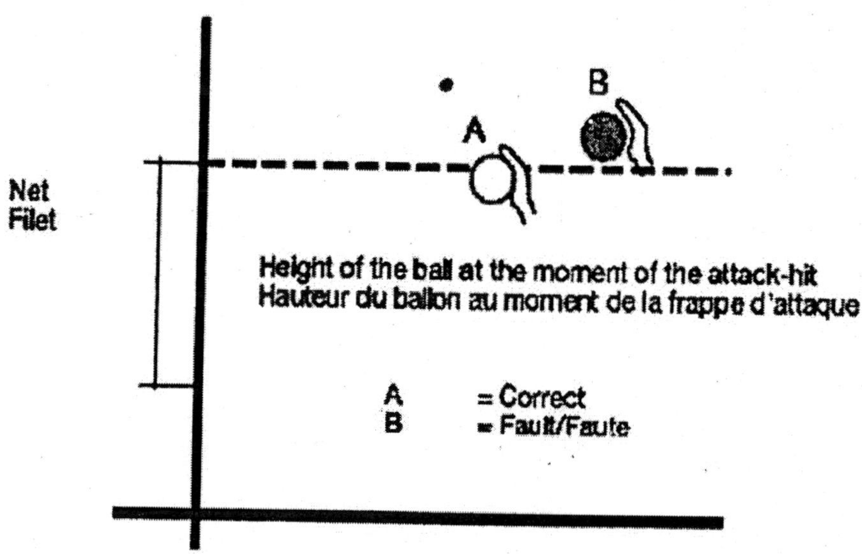
B
A
Net
Filet
Height of the ball at the moment of the attack-hit
Hauteur du ballon au moment de la frappe d'attaque
A = Correct
B = Fault/Faute

the opposing team.

(2) A player hits the ball "out".

(3) A back-row player completes an attack hit from the front zone, if at the moment of the hit the ball is entirely higher than the top of the net.

(4) A player completes an attack hit on the opponent's service, when the ball is in the front zone and entirely higher than the top of the net.

(5) A Libero completes an attack hit if at the moment of the hit the ball is entirely higher than the top of the net.

(6) A player completes an attack hit from higher than the top of the net when the ball is coming from an overhand finger pass by a Libero in his/her front zone.

14. BLOCK

BLOCKING

1. Blocking is the action of players close to the net to intercept the ball coming from the opponent by reaching higher than the top of the net, regardless of the height of the ball contact. Only front-row players are permitted to complete a block, but at the moment of contact with the ball, part of the body must be higher than the top of the net.

Block Attempt

A block attempt is the action of blocking without touching the ball.

A block is completed whenever the ball is touched by a blocker.

Collective Block

A collective block is executed by two or three players close to each other and is completed when one of them touches the ball.

BLOCK CONTACT

Consecutive (quick and continuous) contacts with the ball may occur by one or more blockers provided that the contacts are made during one action.

BLOCKING WITHIN THE OPPONENT'S SPACE

In blocking, the player may place his/her hands and arms beyond the net provided that this action does not interfere with the opponent's play. Thus, it is not permitted to touch the ball beyond the net until an opponent has executed an attack hit.

BLOCK AND TEAM HITS

1. A block contact is not counted as a team hit. Consequently, after a block contact, a team is entitled to three hits to return the ball.

2. The first hit after the block may be executed by any player, including the one who has touched the ball during the block.

BLOCKING THE SERVICE

To block an opponent's service is forbidden.

BLOCKING FAULTS

1. The blocker touches the ball in the OPPONENT'S space either before or simultaneously with the opponent's attack hit.

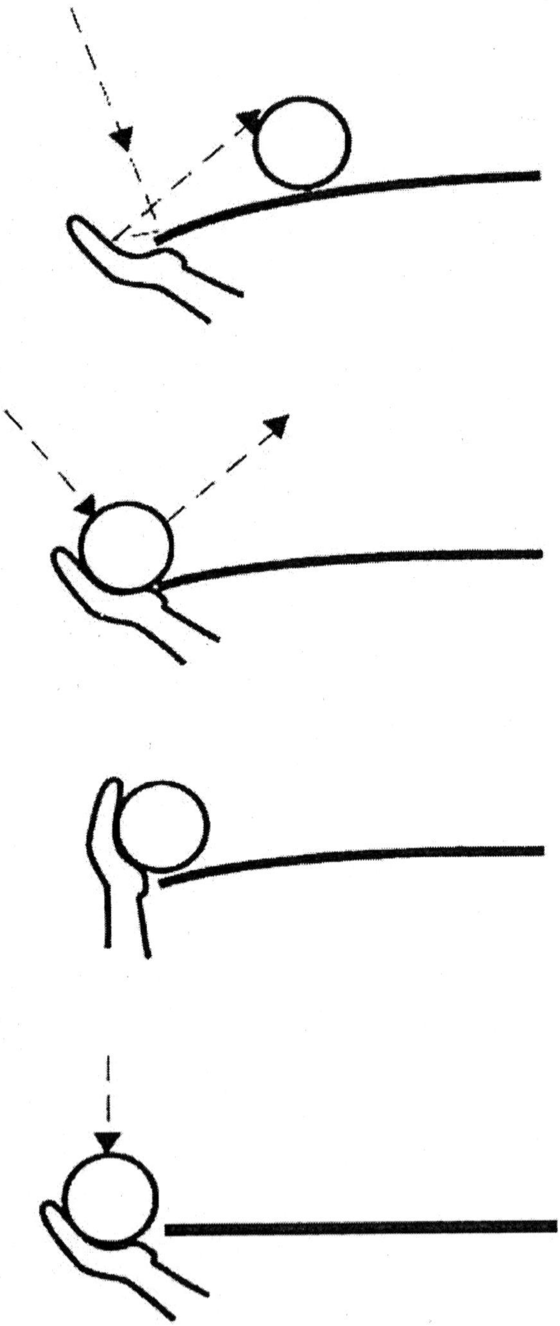

Ball above the net

Ball lower than the top of the net

Ball touches the net

Ball bounces off the net

2. A back-row player or a Libero completes a block or participates in a completed block.

3. Blocking the opponent's service.

4. The ball is sent "out" off the block.

5. Blocking the ball in the opponent's space from outside the antenna.

6. A Libero attempts an individual or collective block.

INTERRUPTIONS, INTERVALS AND DELAYS

15. REGULAR GAME INTERRUPTIONS

Regular game interruptions are TIME-OUTS and SUBSTITUTIONS. An interruption is the time between one completed rally and the 1st referee's whistle for the next service.

NUMBER OF REGULAR GAME INTERRUPTIONS

Each team is entitled to request a maximum of two time-outs and six player substitutions per set.

REQUEST FOR REGULAR GAME INTERRUPTIONS

1. Regular game interruptions may be requested by the coach, or in the absence of the coach by the game captain, and only by them.

The request is made by showing the corresponding hand signal, when the ball is out of play and before the whistle for service.

For FIVB World and Official Competitions it is obligatory to use the buzzer and then the hand signal to request time-out.

2. Substitution before the start of a set is permitted, and should be recorded as a regular substitution in that set.

SEQUENCE OF INTERRUPTIONS

1. Request for one or two time-outs, and one request for player substitution by either team may follow one another, with no need to resume the game.

2. However, a team is not authorized to make consecutive requests for player substitution during the same game interruption. Two or more players may be substituted during the same game interruption.

TIME-OUTS AND TECHNICAL TIME-OUTS

1. All time-outs that are requested last for 30 seconds.

For FIVB World and Official Competitions, in sets 1-4, two additional 60-second "Technical Time-Outs" are applied automatically when the leading team reaches the 8th and 16th points.

In the deciding (5th) set, there are no "Technical Time-Outs"; only two time-outs of 30 seconds duration may be requested by each team.

2 During all time-outs, the players in play must go to the free zone near their bench.

SUBSTITUTION OF PLAYERS

A substitution is the act by which a player, other than the Libero or his/ her replacement player, after being recorded by the scorer, enters the game to occupy the position of another player, who must leave the court at that moment. Substitution requires the referee's authorization.

LIMITATION OF SUBSTITUTIONS

1. Six substitutions is the maximum permitted per team per set. One or more players may be substituted at the same time.

2. A player of the starting line-up, may leave the game, but only once in a set, and re-enter, but only once in a set, and only to his/her previous position in the line-up.

3. A substitute player may enter the game in place of a player of the starting line-up, but only once per set, and he/she can only be substituted by the same starting player.

EXCEPTIONAL SUBSTITUTION

A player (except the Libero) who cannot continue playing due to injury or illness, should be substituted legally. If this is not possible, the team is entitled to make an EXCEPTIONAL substitution, beyond the limits of

An exceptional substitution means that any player who is not on the court at the time of the injury, except the Libero or his/her replacement player, may be substituted into the game for the injured player. The substituted injured player is not allowed to re-enter the match.

An exceptional substitution cannot be counted in any case as a regular substitution.

SUBSTITUTION FOR EXPULSION OR DISQUALIFICATION

An EXPELLED or DISQUALIFIED player must be

substituted immediately through a legal substitution. If this is not possible, the team is declared INCOMPLETE.

ILLEGAL SUBSTITUTION

1. A substitution is illegal, if it exceeds the limitations.

2. When a team has made an illegal substitution and the play has been resumed the following procedure shall apply:

(i) the team is penalized with a point and service to the opponent.

(ii) the substitution is rectified.

(iii) the points scored by the team at fault since the fault was committed are cancelled. The opponent's points remain valid.

SUBSTITUTION PROCEDURE

1. Substitution must be carried out within the substitution zone.

2. A substitution shall only last the time needed for recording the substitution on the score sheet, and allowing entry and exit of the players.

(i) The actual request for substitution is the entrance of the substitute player(s) into the substitution zone, ready to play, during a regular interruption.

If that is not the case, the substitution is not granted and the team is sanctioned for a delay.

The request for substitution is acknowledged and announced by the scorer or second referee, by use of the buzzer or whistle respectively.

For FIVB World and Official Competitions, numbered paddles are used to facilitate the substitution.

If a team intends to make simultaneously more than one substitution, all substitutes must report to the substitution zone at the same time to be considered in the same request. In this case, substitutions must be made in succession, one pair of players after another.

IMPROPER REQUESTS

1. It is improper to request any game interruption:

(i) during a rally or at the moment of, or after the whistle to serve,

(ii) by a non-authorized team member,

(iii) for player substitution before the game has been resumed from a previous substitution by the same team,

(iv) after having exhausted the authorized number of time-outs and player substitutions.

2. The first improper request by a team in the match that does not affect or delay the game shall be rejected without any other consequences.

3. Any further improper request in the match by the same team constitutes a delay.

16. GAME DELAYS

TYPES OF DELAYS

An improper action of a team that defers resumption of the game is a delay and includes, among others:

1. delaying a substitution,

2. prolonging other game interruptions, after having been instructed to resume the game,

3. requesting an illegal substitution,

4. repeating an improper request,

5. delaying the game by a team member.

DELAY SANCTIONS

1. "Delay warning" and "delay penalty" are team sanctions.

(i) Delay sanctions remain in force for the entire match.

(ii) All delay sanctions are recorded on the score sheet.

2. The first delay in the match by a team member is sanctioned with a "DELAY WARNING".

3. The second and subsequent delays of any type by any member of the same team in the same match constitute a fault and are sanctioned with a "DELAY PENALTY": a point and service to the opponent.

4. Delay sanctions imposed before or between sets are applied in the following set.

17. EXCEPTIONAL GAME INTERRUPTIONS

INJURY

1. Should a serious accident occur while the ball is in play, the referee must stop the game immediately and permit medical assistance to enter the court.

The rally is then replayed.

2. If an injured player cannot be substituted, legally or exceptionally, the player is given a 3-minute recovery time, but not more than once for the same player in the match.

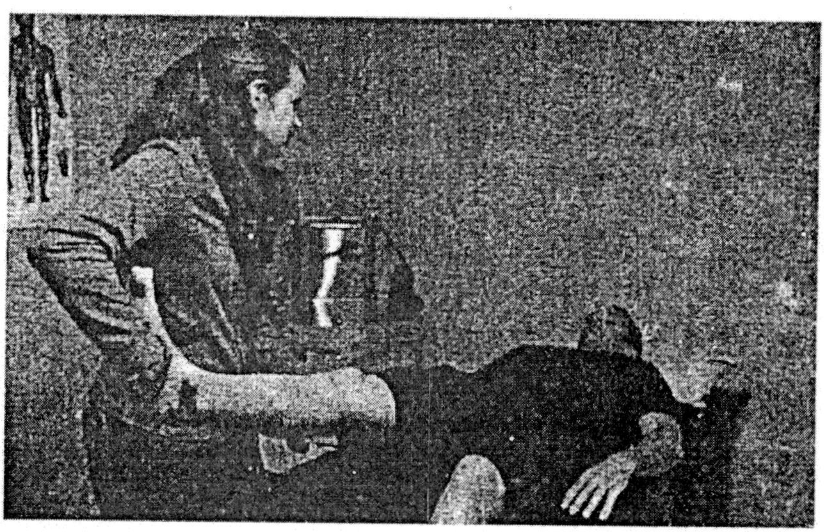

If the player does not recover, his/her team is declared incomplete.

EXTERNAL INTERFERENCE

If there is any external interference during the game, play has to be stopped and the rally is replayed.

PROLONGED INTERRUPTIONS

1. If unforeseen circumstances interrupt the match, the first referee, the organizer and the Control Committee, if there is one, shall decide the measures to be taken to re-establish normal conditions.

2. Should one or several interruptions occur, not exceeding 4 hours in total:

(i) if the match is resumed on the same playing court, the interrupted set shall continue normally with the same score, players and positions. The sets already played will keep their scores;

(ii) if the match is resumed on another playing court, the interrupted set is cancelled and replayed with the same team members and the same starting line-ups. The sets already played will keep their scores.

3. Should one or several interruptions occur, exceeding 4 hours in total, the whole match shall be replayed.

18. INTERVALS AND CHANGE OF COURTS

INTERVALS

An interval is the time between sets. All intervals last three minutes.

During this period of time, the change of courts and line-up registrations of the teams on the score sheet are made.

The interval between the second and the third sets can be extended up to 10 minutes by the competent body at the request of the organizer.

CHANGE OF COURTS

1. After each set, the teams change courts, with the exception of the deciding set.

2. In the deciding set, once the leading team reaches 8 points, the teams change courts without delay and the player positions remain the same.

If the change is not made once the leading team reaches 8 points, it will take place as soon as the error is noticed. The score at the time that the change is made remains the same.

THE LIBERO PLAYER

19. THE LIBERO PLAYER

DESIGNATION OF THE LIBERO

1. Each team has the right to designate from the list of players up to two (2) specialised defensive players: Liberos.

For FIVB and World Competitions for Seniors where a team chooses to have more than twelve (12) players, it is compulsory for the team to designate amongst the list of players two (2) specialised defensive players: "Liberos".

2. All Liberos must be recorded on the score sheet

before the match in the special lines reserved for this.

For FIVB, World and Official Competitions, all Liberos must be recorded on the score sheet before the match only in the special lines reserved for this.

3. One Libero designated by the coach before the start of the match, will be the acting Libero. If there is a second Libero, he/she will act as the reserve Libero.

4. The Libero cannot be either team captain or game captain at the same time as performing the Libero function.

EQUIPMENT

The Libero players must wear a uniform (or jacket/bib for the redesignated Libero) whose jerseys at least must contrast in colour with that of the other members of the team. The Libero uniform may have a different design, but it must be numbered like the rest of the team members.

For FIVB World and Official Competitions the re-designated Libero must wear the same style and colour of jersey as the original Libero, but keep his/her own number.

ACTIONS INVOLVING THE LIBERO

1. The playing actions

(i) The Libero is allowed to replace any player in a back row position.

(ii) He/she is restricted to perform as a back row player and is not allowed to complete an attack hit from anywhere (including playing court and free zone) if at the moment of the contact, the ball is entirely higher than the top of the net.

(iii) He/she may not serve, block or attempt to block.

A player may not complete an attack hit from higher than the top of the net, if the ball is coming from an overhand finger pass by a Libero in his/her front zone. The ball may be freely attacked if the Libero makes the same action from outside his/her front zone.

2. Replacements of players

1. Replacements involving the Libero are not counted as regular substitutions.

They are unlimited, but there must be a completed rally between two Libero replacements (unless due to injury/illness or there is a forced rotation caused by a penalty).

The Libero can only be replaced by the player whom he/she replaced.

2. Replacements must only take place while the ball is out of play and before the whistle for service.

At the start of each set, the Libero cannot enter the court until the second referee has checked the starting line-up.

3. A replacement made after the whistle for service but before the service hit should not be rejected but must be the object of a verbal caution after the end of the rally.

Subsequent late replacements shall result in the play being interrupted immediately and the imposition of a delay sanction. The team to serve next will be determined by the result of the delay sanction.

The Libero and the replacing player may only enter or leave the court by the "Libero Replacement Zone".

The consequences of an illegal Libero replacement are the same as those for a rotational fault.

3. Re-designation of a new Libero:

The coach has the right to exchange the acting Libero with the reserve Libero for any reason, but only once in the match, and only after the regular replacement player has returned to court. This exchange must be recorded in the Remarks section of the score sheet and on the Libero Control sheet.

The original Libero may not re-enter to play for the remainder of the match.

In case of illness or injury to the reserve Libero, the coach may designate as Libero for the remainder of the match any other player (except the original Libero) not on the court at the moment of the re-designation. The team captain may relinquish all leadership privileges to be redesignated as the Libero, if so requested by the coach. Exchanges due to injury or illness of the Libero or re-designated Libero are not counted as replacements.

In the case of a re-designated Libero, the number of the player redesignated as Libero must be recorded on the score sheet remarks section.

PARTICIPANTS' CONDUCT

20. REQUIREMENTS OF CONDUCT

SPORTSMANLIKE CONDUCT

1. Participants must know the "Official Volleyball Rules" and abide by them.

2. Participants must accept referees' decisions with sportsmanlike conduct, without disputing them.

In case of doubt, clarification may be requested only through the game captain.

3. Participants must refrain from actions or attitudes aimed at influencing the decisions of the referees or covering up faults committed by their team.

FAIR PLAY

1. Participants must behave respectfully and courteously in the spirit of FAIR PLAY, not only towards the referees, but also towards other officials, the OPPONENT, team-mates and spectators.

2. Communication between team members during the match is permitted.

21. MISCONDUCT AND ITS SANCTIONS

MINOR MISCONDUCT

Minor misconduct offences are not subject to sanctions. It is the first referee's duty to prevent the teams from approaching the sanctioning level by issuing a verbal or hand signal warning to a team member or to the team through the game captain.

This warning is not a sanction and has no immediate consequences. It should not be recorded on the score sheet.

MISCONDUCT LEADING TO SANCTIONS

Incorrect conduct by a team member towards officials, OPPONENT, team-mates or spectators is classified in three categories according to the seriousness of the offence.

1. Rude conduct: action contrary to good manners or moral principles, or any action expressing contempt.

2. Offensive conduct: defamatory or insulting words or gestures.

3. Aggression: actual physical attack or aggressive or threatening behaviour.

SANCTION SCALE

According to the judgment of the first referee and depending on the seriousness of the offence, the sanctions to be applied and recorded on the score sheet are: Penalty, Expulsion or Disqualification.

The first rude conduct in the match by any team member is penalized with a point and service to the opponent.

Expulsion

1. A team member who is sanctioned by expulsion shall not play for the rest of the set and must remain seated in the penalty area with no other consequences.

An expelled coach loses his/her right to intervene in the set and must remain seated in the penalty area.

2. The first offensive conduct by a team member is sanctioned by expulsion with no other consequences.

3. The second rude conduct in the same match, by

the same team member is sanctioned by expulsion with no other consequences.

Disqualification

1. A team member who is sanctioned by disqualification must leave the Competition Control Area for the rest of the match with no other consequences.

2. The first physical attack or implied or threatened aggression is sanctioned by disqualification with no other consequences.

3. The second offensive conduct in the same match by the same team member is sanctioned by disqualification with no other consequences.

4. The third rude conduct in the same match by the same team member is sanctioned by disqualification with no other consequences.

APPLICATION OF MISCONDUCT SANCTIONS

1. All misconduct sanctions are individual sanctions, remain in force for the entire match and are recorded on the scoresheet.

2. The repetition of misconduct by the same team member in the same match is sanctioned progressively (the team member receives a heavier sanction for each successive offence).

3. Expulsion or disqualification due to offensive conduct or aggression does not require a previous sanction.

MISCONDUCT BEFORE AND BETWEEN SETS

Any misconduct occurring before or between sets is

sanctioned.

SANCTION CARDS

Warning : verbal or hand signal, no card 21.1

Penalty : yellow card 21.3.1

Expulsion: red card 21.3.2

Disqualification: yellow + red card (jointly)

THE REFEREES:
Their Responsibilies and Official Hand Signals

22. REFEREEING CORPS AND PROCEDURES

COMPOSITION

The refereeing corps for a match is composed of the following officials:

- the first referee
- the second referee
- the scorer
- four (two) line judges

For FIVB World and Official Competitions, an assistant scorer is compulsory.

PROCEDURES

1. Only the first and second referees may blow a whistle during the match:

(i) the first referee gives the signal for the service that

LOCATION OF REFEREEING CORPS AND THEIR ASSISTANTS

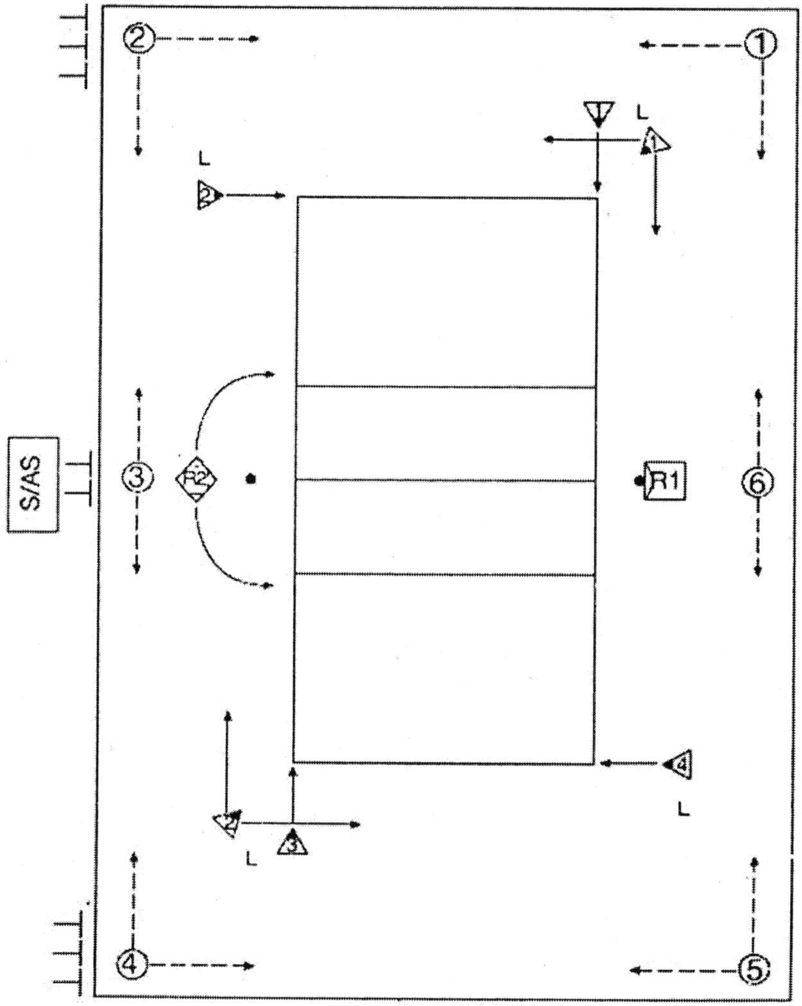

R1 = First Referee - Premier arbitre

R2 = Second Referee - Second arbitre

S/AS = Scorer/Assistant Scorer - Marqueur/Marqueur assistant

= Linesjudges - Juges de ligne (numbers 1-4 or 1-2 / numérotés 1-4 ou 1-2)

④ = Ball Retrievers - Ramasseurs de ballon (numbers 1-6 / numérotés 1-6)

= Floor Moppers - Balayeurs et Essuyeurs

begins the rally;

(ii) the first and second referees signal the end of the rally, provided that they are sure that a fault has been committed and they have identified its nature.

2. They may blow the whistle when the ball is out of play to indicate that they authorize or reject a team request.

3. Immediately after the referee's whistle to signal the completion of the rally, they have to indicate with the official hand signals:

(i) If the fault is whistled by the first referee, he/she will indicate in order:

a) the team to serve,

b) the nature of the fault,

c) the player(s) at fault (if necessary).

The second referee will follow the first referee's hand signals by repeating them.

(ii) If the fault is whistled by the second referee, he/she will indicate:

a) the nature of the fault

b) the player at fault (if necessary)

c) the team to serve following the hand signal of the first referee.

In this case, the first referee does not show either the nature of the fault or the player at fault, but only the team to serve.

(iii) In the case of an attack hit fault by back row or

Libero players, both referees indicate.

(iv) In the case of a double fault both referees indicate in order

a) the nature of the fault

b) the players at fault (if necessary)

c) the team to serve as directed by the first referee

23. FIRST REFEREE

LOCATION

The first referee carries out his/her functions seated or standing on a referee's stand located at one end of the net. His/her view must be approximately 50 cm above the net.

AUTHORITY

1. The first referee directs the match from the start until the end. He/ she has authority over all members of the refereeing corps and the members of the teams.

During the match the first referee's decisions are final. He/she is authorized to overrule the decisions of other members of the refereeing corps, if it is noticed that they are mistaken.

The first referee may even replace a member of the refereeing corps who is not performing his/her functions properly.

2. The first referee also controls the work of the ball retrievers, floor wipers and moppers.

3. The first referee has the power to decide any matter involving the game including those not provided for in

the Rules.

4. The first referee shall not permit any discussion about his/her decisions.

However, at the request of the game captain, the first referee will give an explanation on the application or interpretation of the Rules upon which he/she has based the decision.

If the game captain does not agree with the explanation of the first referee and chooses to protest against such decision, he/she must immediately reserve the right to file and record this protest at the conclusion of the match. The first referee must authorize this right of the game captain.

5. The first referee is responsible for determining before and during the match whether the playing area equipment and the conditions meet playing requirements.

RESPONSIBILITIES

1. Prior to the match, the first referee:

(i) inspects the conditions of the playing area, the balls and other equipment,

(ii) performs the toss with the team captains.

(iii) controls the teams' warming-up.

2. During the match, the first referee is authorized:

(i) to issue warnings to the teams,

(ii) to sanction misconduct and delays,

(iii) to decide upon:

a) the faults of the server and of the positions of the serving team, including the screen.

b) the faults in playing the ball.

c) the faults above the net and at its upper part.

d) the attack hit faults of the Libero and back-row players.

e) the completed attack hit made by a player on a ball above the net height coming from an overhand pass with fingers by the Libero in his/her front zone.

f) the ball crossing completely the lower space under the net.

g) the completed block by back row players or the attempted block by the Libero.

3. At the end of the match, he/she checks the score sheet and signs it.

24. SECOND REFEREE

LOCATION

The second referee performs his/her functions standing outside the playing court near the post, on the opposite side facing the first referee.

AUTHORITY

1. The second referee is the assistant of the first referee, but has also his/her own range of jurisdiction.

Should the first referee become unable to continue his/her work, the second referee may replace the first referee.

2. The second referee may, without whistling, also signal faults outside his/her range of jurisdiction, but may not insist on them to the first referee.

3. The second referee controls the work of the scorer(s).

4. The second referee supervises the team members on the team bench and reports their misconduct to the first referee.

5. The second referee controls the players in the warm-up areas.

6. The second referee authorizes the interruptions, controls their duration and rejects improper requests.

7. The second referee controls the number of time-outs and substitutions used by each team and reports the 2nd time-out and 5th and 6th substitutions to the first referee and the coach concerned.

8. In the case of an injury of a player, the second referee authorizes an exceptional substitution or grants a 3 minute recovery time.

9. The second referee checks the floor condition, mainly in the front zone. He/she also checks, during the match, that the balls still fulfil the regulations.

10. The second referee supervises the team members in the penalty areas and reports their misconduct to the first referee.

RESPONSIBILITIES

1. At the start of each set, at the change of courts in the deciding set and whenever necessary, he/she checks that the actual positions of the players on the court correspond to those on the line-up sheets.

2. During the match, the second referee decides, whistles and signals:

(i) penetration into the opponent's court, and the space under the net,

(ii) positional faults of the receiving team,

(iii) the faulty contact of the player with the net at its lower part or with the antenna on his/her side of the court,

(iv) the completed block by back row players or the attempted block by the Libero; or the attack hit fault by back row players or by the Libero

(v) the contact of the ball with an outside object;

(vi) the contact of the ball with the floor when the first referee is not in position to see the contact;

(vii) the ball that crosses the net totally or partly outside of the crossing space to the opponent court or contacts the antenna on his/her side of the court;

3. At the end of the match, he/ she signs the score sheet.

25. SCORER

LOCATION

The scorer performs his/her functions seated at the

scorer's table on the opposite side of the court facing the first referee.

RESPONSIBILITIES

He/she keeps the score sheet according to the Rules, co-operating with the second referee.

He/she uses a buzzer or other sound device to notify irregularities or give signals to the referees on the basis of his/her responsibilities.

1. Prior to the match and set, the scorer:

(i) registers the data of the match and teams, including the name and number of the Libero player, according to the procedures in force, and obtains the signatures of the captains and the coaches ;

2. records the starting line-up of each team from the line-up sheet;

If he/she fails to receive the line-up sheets on time, he/she immediately notifies this fact to the second referee.

2. During the match, the scorer:

(i) records the points scored 6.1

(ii) controls the serving order of each team and indicates any error to the referees immediately after the service hit;

(iii) Is empowered to acknowledge and announce requests for player substitutions by use of the buzzer, controlling their number; and records the substitutions and time-outs, informing the second referee;

(iv) notifies the referees of a request for interruption

that is out of order;

(v) announces to the referees the ends of the sets, and the scoring of the 8th point in the deciding set;

(vi) records any sanctions and improper requests;

(vii) records all other events as instructed by the second referee, i.e., exceptional substitutions, recovery time, prolonged interruptions, external interference, etc.

(viii) controls the interval between sets

3. At the end of the match, the scorer:

(i) records the final result;

(ii) in the case of protest, with the previous authorization of the first referee, writes or permits the team/game captain to write on the scoresheet a statement on the incident protested.

(iii) after signing the scoresheet him/herself, obtains the signatures of the team captains and then the referees.

26. ASSISTANT SCORER

LOCATION

The assistant scorer performs his/her functions seated beside the scorer at the scorer's table

RESPONSIBILITIES

He/she records the replacements involving the Libero.

He/she assists with the administrative duties of the scorer's work. Should the scorer become unable to continue his/her work, the assistant scorer substitutes for the scorer.

1. Prior to the match and set, the assistant scorer:

(i) prepares the Libero control sheet,

(ii) prepares the reserve scoresheet.

2. During the match, the assistant scorer:

(i) records the details of the Libero replacements,

(ii) notifies the referees of any fault of the Libero replacement, by using the buzzer

(iii) starts and ends the timing of Technical Time-out,

(iv) operates the manual scoreboard on the scorer's table,

(v) checks that the scoreboards agree

(vi) if necessary, updates the reserve scoresheet and gives it to the scorer.

3. At the end of the match, the assistant scorer:

(i) signs the Libero control sheet and submits it for checking;

(ii) signs the scoresheet.

27. LINE JUDGES

LOCATION

If only two line judges are used, they stand at the corners of the court closest to the right hand of each referee, diagonally at 1 to 2 m from the corner.

Each one of them controls both the end line and sideline on his/her side.

For FIVB World and Official Competitions, it is

compulsory to have four line judges.

They stand in the free zone at 1 to 3 m from each corner of the court, on the imaginary extension of the line that they control.

RESPONSIBILITIES

1. The line judges perform their functions by using

flags (40 × 40 cm) to signal:

1. the ball "in" and "out" whenever the ball lands near their line(s),

2. the touches of "out" balls by the team receiving the ball,

3. the ball touching the antenna, the served ball crossing the net outside the crossing space, etc.,

4. any player (except the server) stepping outside of

his/her court at the moment of the service hit,

5. the foot faults of the server,

6. any contact with the antenna on their side of the court by any player during his/her action of playing the ball or interfering with the play,

7. ball crossing the net outside the crossing space into opponent's court or touching the antenna on his/her side of the court.

At the first referee's request, a line judge must repeat his/her signal.

28. OFFICIAL SIGNALS

REFEREES' HAND SIGNALS

The referees must indicate with the official hand signal the reason for their whistle (nature of the fault whistled or the purpose of the interruption authorized). The signal has to be maintained for a moment and, if it is indicated with one hand, the hand corresponds to the side of the team which has made the fault or the request.

LINE JUDGES' FLAG SIGNALS

The line judges must indicate with the official flag signal the nature of the fault called, and maintain the signal for a moment.

Point

Winner of the rally. One finger raised on the side of the court that won the rally.

Ball in bounds

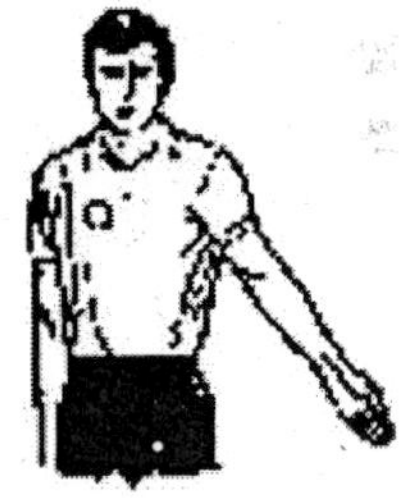

Pointing to the area of the court where the ball landed.

Out of bounds

Ball is out of bounds, outside antenna or player illegally in adjacent court.

Touch

Ball is out of bounds after contacting a player.

4 Contacts

Four fingers up. You only get 3 contacts.

Carry

Held, thrown or carried ball. Too much contact time.

Double Hit

Two fingers up. Ball contacted more than once by a player. The block does not count.

Begin Service

The official indicates that the server may now serve.

Out of Rotation

At the time of service you must not overlap the person directly next to you.

Back Row Attack

Attacking the ball above the net and leaving from in front of the 3 meter line.

Sanction Card

A yellow card is a warning. A red card is a point. Red and yellow together is an ejection.

Change Sides

Between games or halfway through a deciding game.

Game Over

Same for the end of the match.

LINE-JUDGES OFFICIAL FLAG SIGNALS

BALL "IN"

Point down with flag.

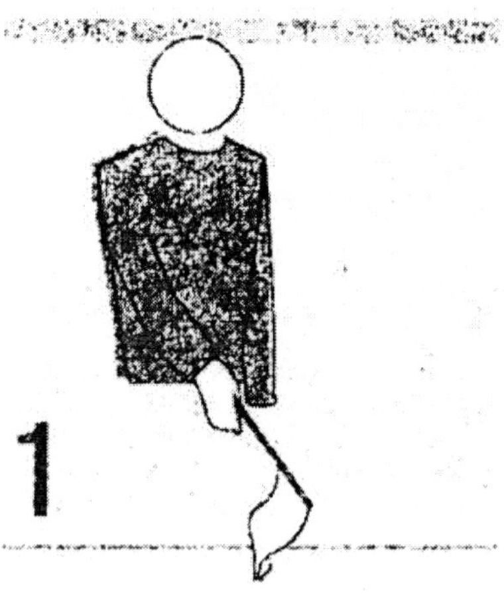

BALL "OUT"

Raise flag vertically.

BALL TOUCHED

Raise flag and touch the top with the palm of the free hand.

CROSSING SPACE FAULTS, BALL TOUCHED AN OUTSIDE OBJECT, OR FOOT FAULT BY ANY PLAYER DURING SERVICE

Wave flag over the head and point to the antenna or the respective line

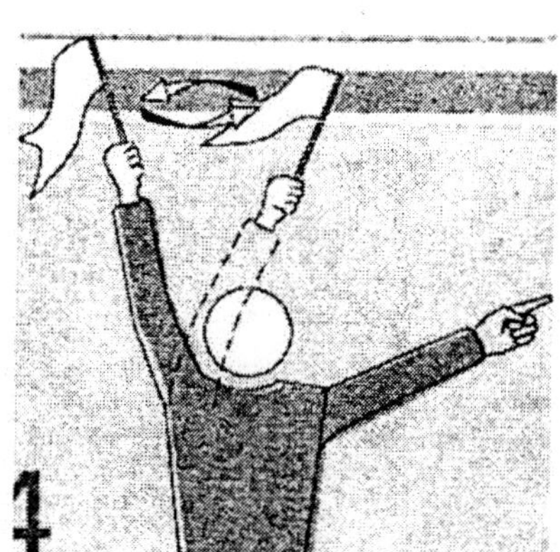

JUDGEMENT IMPOSSIBLE

Raise and cross both arms and hands in front of the chest.

REVIEW OF VOLLEYBALL RULES

PLAYING SURFACE

a. Play should be conducted only on a flat, horizontal and uniform surfaced area which should be safe for

players. Play should not be conducted on rough or slippery surfaces. Only surface of wood or synthetic surface should be used in FIVB World and official Competitions. Any above mentioned surfaces can be used, however, they should be approved by FIVB.

ii. Surface of light colour should be used in indoor courts.

iii. In FIVB World and Official Competitions, lines of white colour should be drawn, whereas in playing court and free zone lines of other colours should be drawn.

Playing Area

Playing court and Free Zone jointly are termed as Playing Area. This area should be of rectangular shape and have symmetry.

Lines

a. Boundary Lines: Playing court should be marked by two sidelines and two end lines. These lines should be drawn inside the dimensions of Playing Court.

b. Attack Line: To mark the front zone an attack line should be drawn on each court. Rear edge of this line should be drawn 3 m back from axis of centre line.

c. Centre-Line: To divide the playing court into equal parts, centre line is drawn. This line divides the court into two parts measuring 9×9 m each.

All lines should have a width of 5m, which should have a light colour, but different from floor's colour and any other lines.

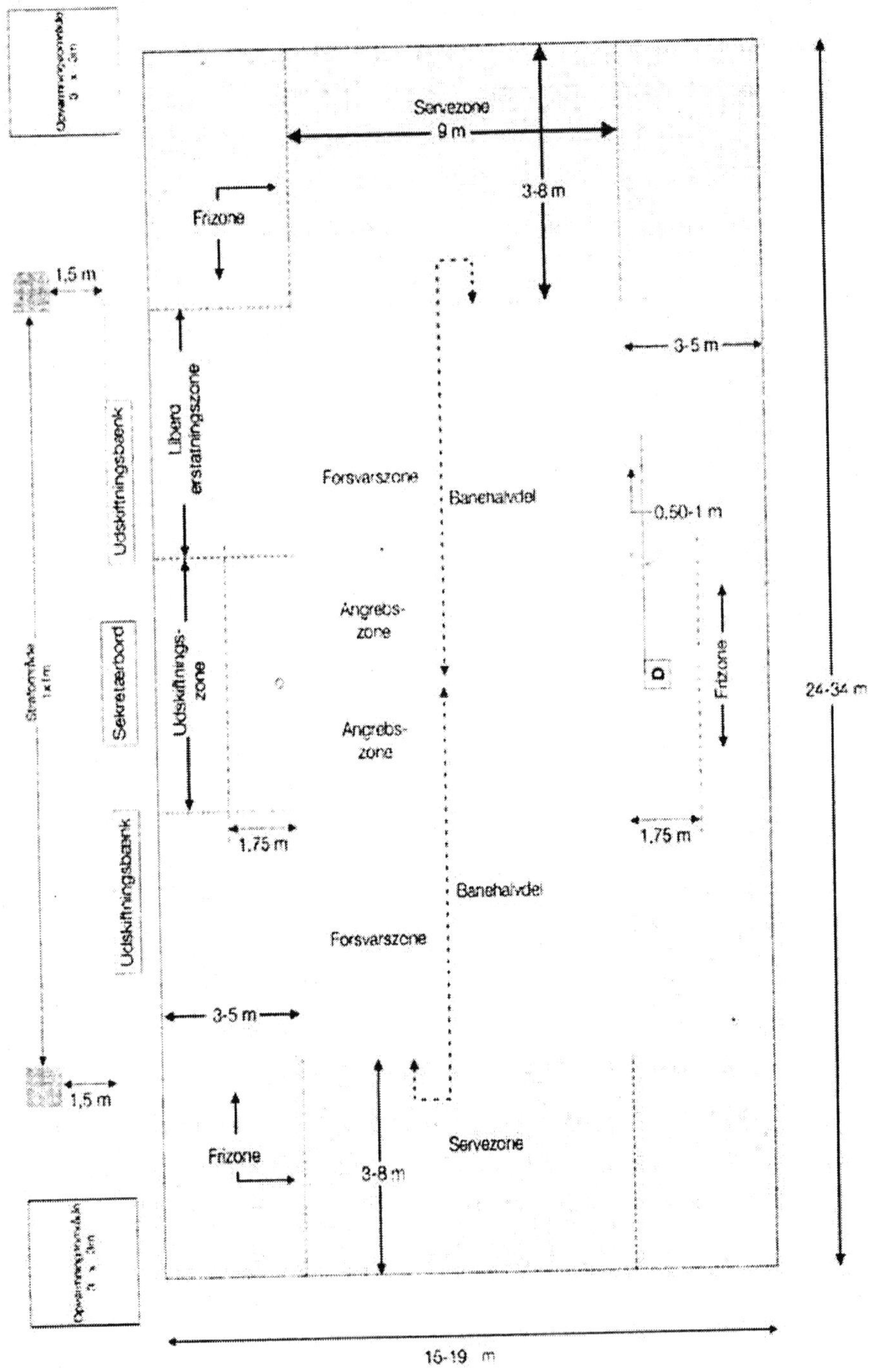
Servezone
9 m
3-8 m
Frizone
1,5 m
3-5 m
Libero erstatningszone
Udskiftningsbænk
Forsvarszone
Banehalvdel
0,50-1 m
Angrebs-zone
Angrebs-zone
Sekretærbord
Udskiftnings-zone
D
Frizone
24-34 m
1,75 m
1,75 m
Banehalvdel
Udskiftningsbænk
Forsvarszone
3-5 m
1,5 m
Frizone
3-8 m
Servezone
15-19 m

Dimensions

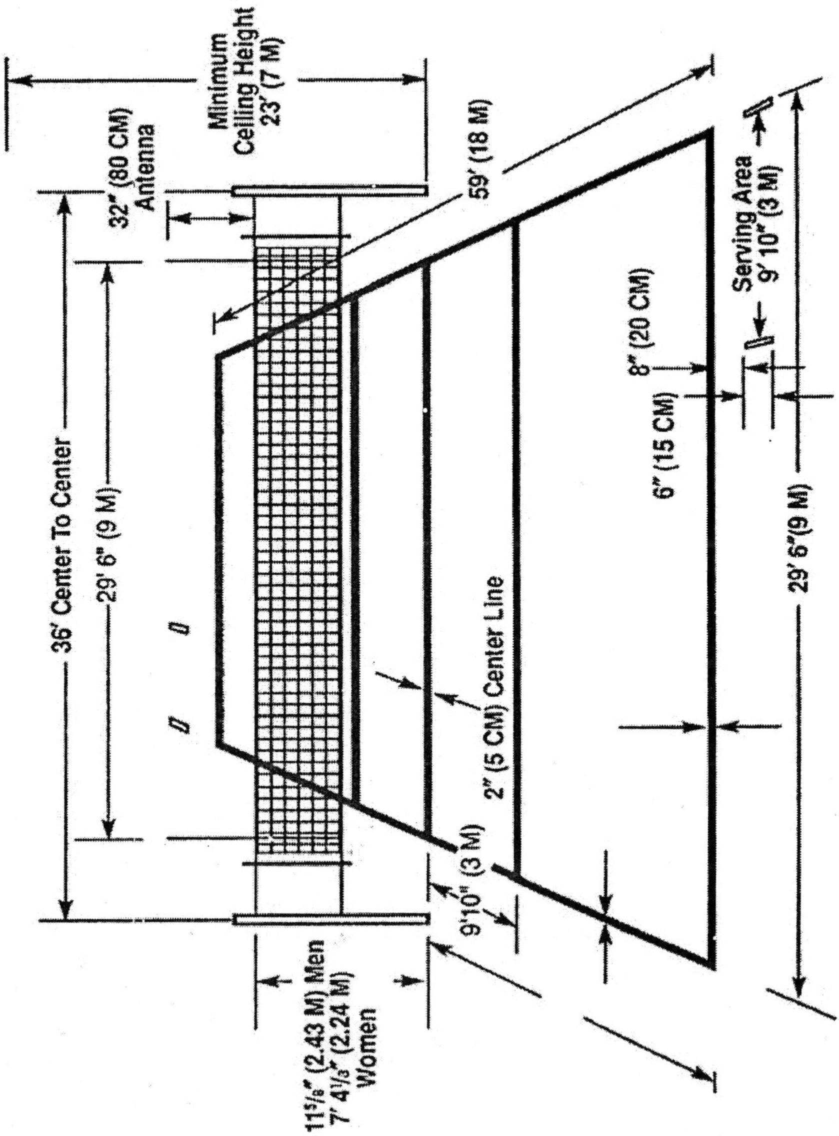
Minimum Ceiling Height 23' (7 M)
32" (80 CM) Antenna
59' (18 M)
36' Center To Center
29' 6" (9 M)
2" (5 CM) Center Line
8" (20 CM)
6" (15 CM)
Serving Area 9' 10" (3 M)
29' 6"(9 M)
9'10" (3 M)
7' 11⅝" (2.43 M) Men
7' 4⅓" (2.24 M) Women

Playing court should have a rectangular shape which should be 18m long and 9m wide. It should be surrounded by a free zone which should have a width of 3m.

Space above the playing area which is without any obstruction is known as Free Playing Space. This space should be situated at a height of 7 m from playing surface.

In FIVB World Competitions these specifications can change. Free zone should situates 5m from sidelines and 8m from end lines, whereas free playing surface should situate at a height of 12.5m from playing surface.

Weather

Minimum temperature should not be less than 10°C or 50°F. However, for FIVB Competitions minimum temperature should not be less than 16°C and maximum temperature not less than 25°C.

Lighting

There should be proper lighting provision on court. In FIVB World and Official Competitions lighting of 1000

to 1500 luxes measuring at a height of 1m from playing surface should be done.

THE NET

Structure of Net

Net of 1m width and 9.50 length should be used in play. Net should be made of 10cm square black mesh. A 5cm wide horizontal band should be there on its top, which should be made up of two-fold white canvas sewn along its full length. For keeping its top taught, each extreme end of band should have a hole through which

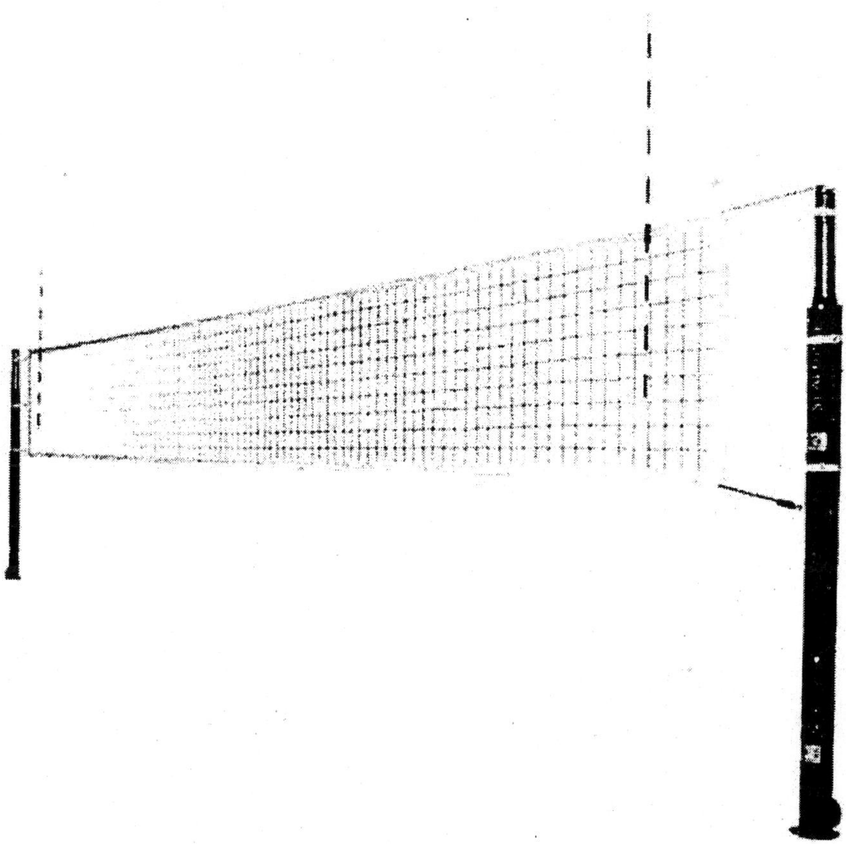

a cord can be passed which fastened the band to the posts. To fasten the net to posts and keeping its top taught, a flexible cable should be there in band.

To fasten net to the posts and to keep its lower part taut, a rope .should be threaded through meshes at its bottom.

Height

Over the centre line a net should be placed vertically in such a way that its top is set at a height of 2.43 m for men and 2.24 m for women.

Height of net should be measured from centre of the court. It should not be placed at more height that prescribed.

Vertical Side Markers

At each end of net vertical to side lines and centre line two movable tapes of 5cm width should be marked. Two flexible stick should be fastened to the net which should be parallel to tapes and just outside them. These sticks should be placed at a distance of 9.40 m from each other. These sticks should have a length of 1.80 m and a radius of 5mm. These should be made of fibreglass or similar material and should extend to 80 cm above top the net. These should have rods of contrasting colour having sections of 10cm width.

At a distance of 50cm from side lines posts supporting net should be placed.

Volleyball Post

i. Posts should have rounded shape. No wire should be used to fix it to ground.

i. At a distance of .50-1.00 m outside the sideline posts should be placed. These posts are placed to support the net, which should have a height of 2.55m. These should be flexible.

Antenna

An Antenna is a flexible rod of fibreglass or similar material. It should have a length of 1.80m and diameter of 10mm. These should be fastened at outer edge of each side-band, and should be placed on opposite sides of net.

Over the net top 80 cm of each antenna should extend which should be marked with 10 cm stripes of

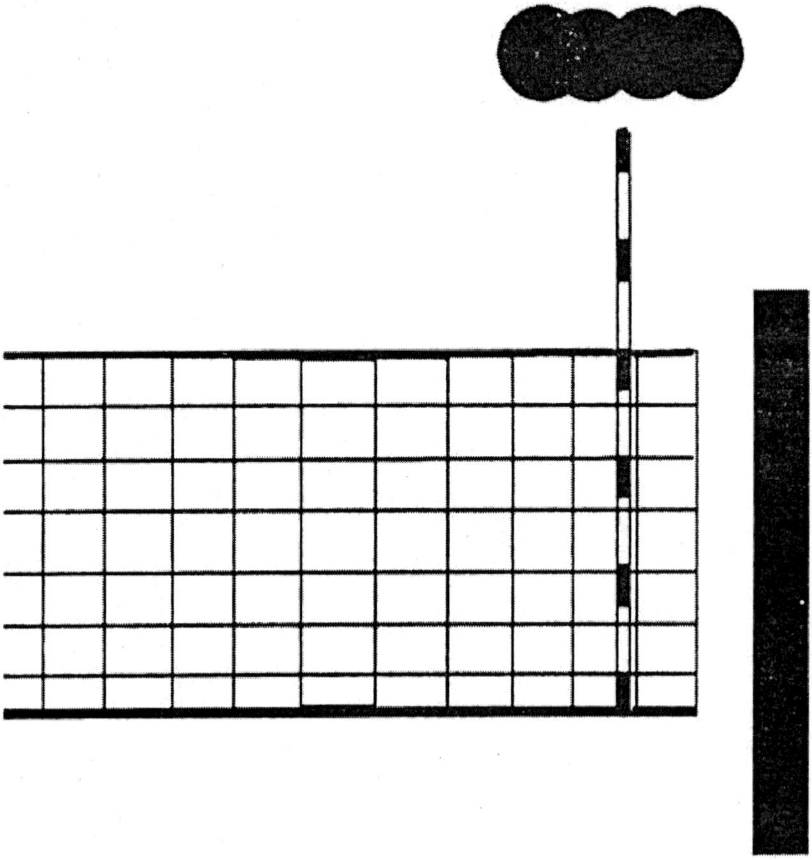

contrasting colour.

These are considered to be part of the net which limits the crossing space.

Bali

Ball should have spherical shape. It should be made up of flexible leather or synthetic leather case inside which a bladder of rubber or similar material should be placed. It can be of a single colour or of multiple colours.

Weight of ball should be between 260 to 280 g and

circumference between 65 to 67cm. Its inside pressure should be between 0.30 to 0.325 kg/cm^2.

Features

Circumference, weight, pressure, type, colour etc. of all balls used in a match should be same.

In FIVB World and Official Competitions, only FIVB approved balls should be used.

Three-Balls System

3 balls should be used in FIVB World and Official Competitions. 6 ball retrievers should be stationed, one at each corner of free-zone and one behind each referee.

Rights and Duties of Players

a. All players should have thorough knowledge of rules of game.

b. Only team captain has the right to interact with referee. Captain will also act as spokesman for his players. He can also address the umpire for matters relating to his duties.

Penalties

i. A penalty can be awarded for any serious offence, by result of which offending team can loose the service or opposing team can get a point. A player can be disqualified from the match who commits a foul for more than once.

Player making bad comments to officials, opponents or spectators can be disqualified by referee without any prior warning.

ii. Player should be warned who is either talking to his opponent, spectator, or officials or shouting during play.

Personal warning should be issued to player committing the same offence after being warned. Loss of Service of winning of point to opponent can result from this Personal Warning. This personal warning should be noted down on Score Sheet.

Behaviour of Players, Substitutes and Coaches

Players are not allowed to behave in any of following way:

i. to make comments on opponents;

ii. to make uncivil comments on officials;

iii. to go out of court during an interruption of play without taking permission of referee;

iv. to disagree with decisions of officials;

v. to insist an official to change the decision to act in an uncivil way;

vi. to clap or shout at time of contact with ball and particular during service reception with an object to distract the referee in his judgement related to handing of ball;

vii. to receive any kind of coaching from his coach during play.

Equipments of Players

Following different equipments are used by players:

a. A jersey, shorts, shoes and socks are included in uniform of players. These should be neat and clean.

b. Players should wear light, pliable and flat shoes

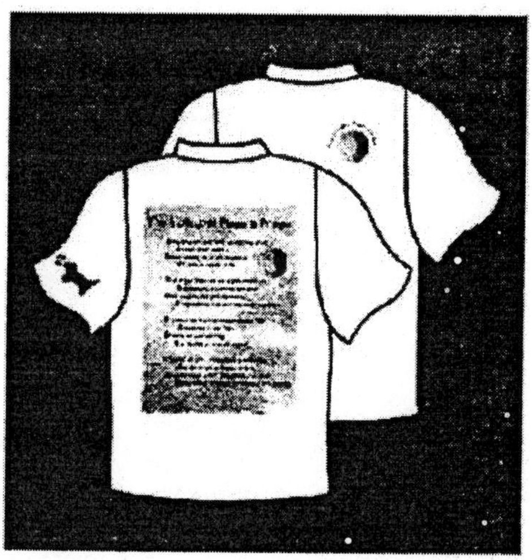

which should be of rubber or leather.

c. Jerseys of all the players should be numbered through 1 to 8. These numbers should be of different contrasting colour than colour of jersey and should be placed a height of 10 cm on chest and at 15 cm on back.

Non-Permissible Objects and Uniforms

a. No player is allowed to wear any harmful object or object which can provide any kind of advantage to any player;

b. Colour of uniform of all players of a team should be same. Jersey without number should not be used.

Variations

a. If by chance colour of uniform of both teams are same, home team is required to change its dress. If a neutral site is involved, the team listed first on the score-sheet shall change uniforms.

b. Players can play in their training suits if first referee authorise to do so because of cold weather. This is possible only when they are of same colour, design and numbered properly.

c. First referee can authorise players to:

i. play without shoes;

ii. change their wet jerseys between sets or after substitution.

Team Captain

Team captain is required to do the following things before commencement of match:

i. to sign the scoresheet;

ii. to act as representative of his at time of toss.

At end of match he will thanks the referees and signs the score sheet to ratify the outcome.

Rights and Liabilities of the Team Captain

i. As mentioned earlier he will act as a spokesman of his players, so he will submit any question or request of his players to the referee;

ii. He can make a request to referee to change his uniform and any equipment;

iii. He can ask first referee to verify the net, floor, ball and positions of opponents;

iv. He can demand legal interruptions in the game.

Fundamental Liabilities

a. All the participants are required to agree with decisions of referee. If they have any kind of doubt captain of team can submit a request for clarification of his judgment.

b. All the participants should have complete knowledge of rules of the game;

c. All participants should behave in a respectful manner with all officials and opponents.

d. All participants should play with a sportsmanlike spirit.

e. Participants does not attempt to act in such a manner which will change the decision of official;

f. No player who is out of game should provide any kind of instruction or advice to player on field;

g. No player is allowed to make delay in the game;

h. It is the responsibility of team captain's and coach to maintain their team in discipline;

i. No player, other than captain can request for clarification from referee.

Liabilities of the Coach

a. He is required to hand over a completed and signed Line-Up Sheet to referee before beginning of each set;

b. Before game, he will note down and verify the names and numbers of players on score sheet and will sign it;

c. He can sit on player's bench near the scorer during the match.

d. Before match he can direct warm-up sessions of his players.

Liabilities of the Assistant Coach

a. If because of any reason coach is not able to present at field, his assistant can perform his responsibilities. For this, permission of first referee should be taken.

b. He can sit on bench of player.

Team Coaches, Manager and Captains

The coach or captain has the right to request a time-out substitution. During a time-out he has the right to speak to players but may not enter the court.

Team

Number of players

i. Not more than 6 players can be included in a team. However, 6 substitutes are also allowed. Before commencement of game names and numbers of all players should be recorded properly on Score Sheet. Player whose name does not appear in Score Sheet will not allowed to participate in the game.

ii. A player cannot be substituted for more than once in any set. As soon as substitute enters the court, substituted player should leave the court. Further, substitute can be replaced only be player substituted previously.

If the team becomes incomplete as a result of a player being sent off and all normal substitutions have been carried out, the team loses the set in progress but retains the points it has scored.

Players Substituted

Captain or coach of the team can request referee or umpire to substitute any player during period ball is dead.

Upto 6 substitutions can be made in each set. Substitute is required to report scorer in playing strip before joining the game, and should enter into court as soon as he is ordered to do so. If he does not enter court immediately after receiving order to do so, a time out should be charted out. A team can lose the service or opponent can be

Referee will be indicated by captain or coach of team about number of players involved in the substitution. After completion of substitution a team cannot demand new substitution before resumption of play and dead ball again.

Legal Substitution

a. Any player can be substituted only at time when ball is dead and before blow of whistle for service;

b. Following specifications should be kept in mind related to substitution of players:

i. Only for once player of starting line-up can leave the game Player of starting line-up is allowed to leave the game only for one time.

Procedure for Legal Substitutions

Following procedure should be followed to substitute a player:

a. Referee has the right to accept or reject the request of substitution;

b. Coaches cannot speak to their players at time of substitution;

c. If request of substitution is accepted by referee, substitute player will enter from side line by raising his hand or numbered cards. At the same time player having same number of card should stand in front of his substitute. On signal of second referee, substitute will enter into the court and will take numbered cards from substitute.

Substitution Faults

In following conditions a team is considered to have made the substitution fault:

a. if it requests an illegal substitution for second time when it has already exhausted its 2 time-outs;

b. if substitute does not enter the court immediately after receiving signal from referee or he is not present in substitution zone and team has already exhausted its allowable time-outs;

c. if any team makes an illegal substitution. In this condition referee is required to penalise this foul, disallow the substitution and deduct the points from team's score.

Compulsory Substitution

In following conditions a team has to substitute his player:

a. if any of its player get injured, even if team has exhausted its allowable substitutions;

b. an expelled player should be substituted legally.

Location of Players

Following provisions should be followed during serving of ball:

Players of both teams must be within their courts in two lines of three players, taking positions as follows:

The three players at the net are front line players, occupying from right to left, position 2, 3 and 4, while the three players in the back are back line players, occupying from right to left, positions 1, 6 and 5.

The positions of the players on the court must conform to the rotational order recorded on the score sheet; namely:

In the front line, 3 must be between 2 and 4, and in front of 6. In the back line, 6 must be between 1 and 5, and behind. Consequently, 2 must be in front of 1, and 4 must be in front of 5. Once the line-up sheet has been given to the scorer no change of line-up is authorized, unless there has been an error or omission by the scorer.

Any discrepancy between the line-up sheet and the actual position of the players on the court must be corrected before the start of the game according to the line-up sheet, without penalty. However, if one or more players on the court is not identified on the line-up sheet, the team is requested to correct the mistake according to the line-up sheet without penalty.

But if the coach of the team wishes to keep the players on the court, he must requested the substitutions of the player. In this case, this team will be charged the necessary substitution.

In following manner position of players are determined and controlled by position of their feet contacting the ground:

i. Each right or left player should have any part of his foot closer to respective side line. Feet of centre player who belongs to same line of players should have his foot farther from these players;

ii. Each front line player should have any part of his foot near to centre line, and foot of his corresponding backline teammate should be farther from him.

Players are free to move about and to have any position on their own court and free zone after serving of ball.

Within their playing area, players can move anywhere except under net on court of their opponent.

Throughout the set rotation order should be same as indicated by score sheet. Rotation order can be changed but only at beginning of each set which should be recorded on Score Sheet.

Mistake in Locating Players

Play should be interrupted as soon as any player of the team is found to be out of his position. All points which team made in wrong position should not be taken into consideration. A side-out should be called out if team at time of discovery of same is serving. Points scored by opponent should remain unchanged.

If time of occurrence of error cannot be determined, team concerned will re-start the game after taking the correct position. Defaulted team can be penalised by loss of service or by awarding of point to opponent.

Positional Fault

If at time of service any player of a team is not position on his authorised placed, he is considered to have committed the Positional Fault.

Consequences of a Positional Fault

i. Serving Foul of server should be considered to be decisive to positional fault if he commits this foul at moment he hits the ball.

ii. In following way a Positional Fault should be penalised:

a. In order to determine points scored by team during foul scorer is required to determine the exact time when foul was committed.

b. With discovery of fouls all or concerned player should take proper place;

c. Penalty should be awarded if points scored by team during foul cannot be determined.

Selection of Captain

a. A team consists of a captain who is regarded as sportsman and representative of team;

b. Coach or captain will select other captain out of existing players if because of any reason he cannot continue to play;

c. Captain should wear a ribbon or strip which will distinguish him from other players. This strip should measure 8cm × 2cm and should have different colour from jersey. It should be placed on left side of captain's uniform. Player's Strip

i. Through 8 to 15 players' jerseys should be numbered. These numbers should be placed at a height of 15cm on back.

In international matches, the captain shall wear a badge on the left side of his chest, measuring 8cm. by 1.5cm. in a different colour to that of the jersey.

ii. A player should wear a jersey, shorts, and light shoes. They cannot wear any headgear or any kind of injurious article. Referee can allow any player to play barefooted, if player makes any request for the same.

iii. Uniform of all players of a team should be same. They can wear training suits if referee allow them because of cold weather.

Officials and their Duties

Presence of following official is must in a game:

1 referee;

1 umpire;

1 scorer;

2 linesmen.

Umpire

Umpire will sit on that side of court from which he can face-out the referee properly.

Following are included in duties of umpire:

a. He is required to indicate when ball touches vertical side markers and goes outside them;

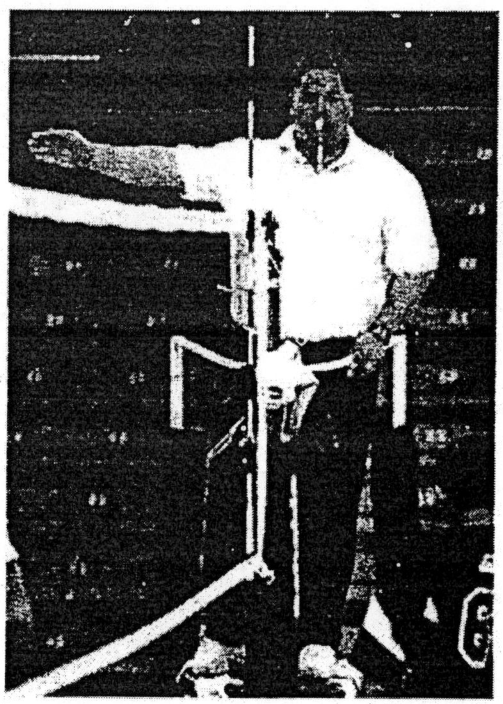

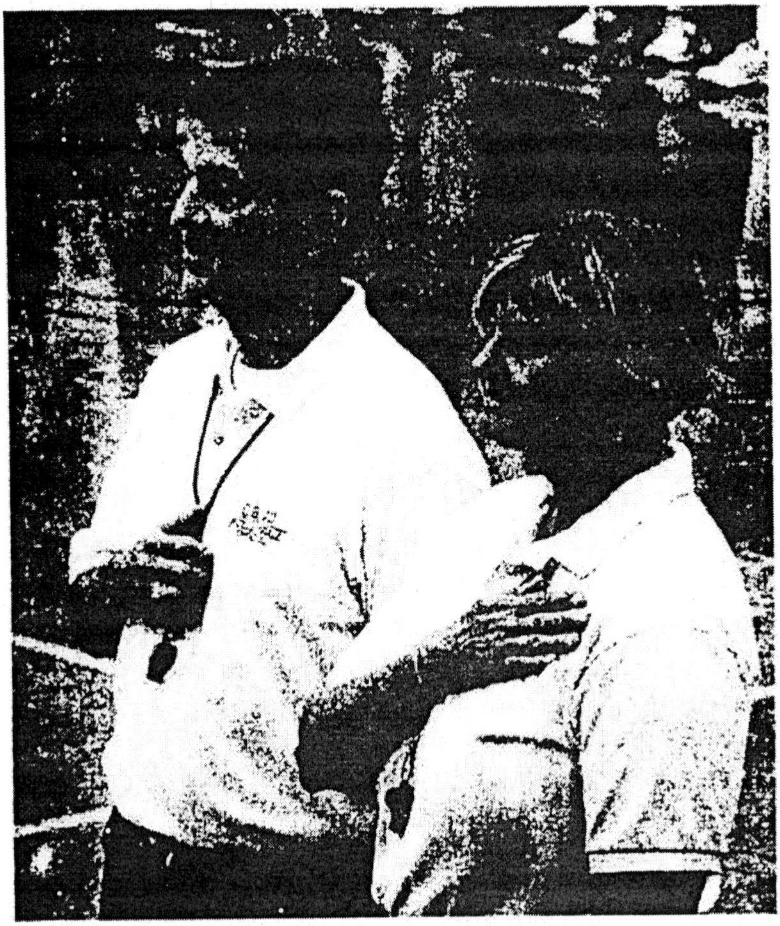

b. Whenever a player crosses the centre line or has illegally played the ball within the attack zone, he should blow the whistle.

c. He will give his judgment when ball contacts with the net, except those over or near the top of the net;

d. He supervises the conduct of coaches and substitutes on the bench.

e. He times the duration of the times-out.

f. He watches for contact of the ball with any foreign objects.

g. He verifies at the beginning of each set that the initial positions of each team correspond exactly to the order of rotation as shown on the score sheet.

h. He gives his opinion to the referee in all matters, when requested.

i. He checks that the rotational order and positions of the receiving team are correct at the time of each service.

j. He calls the attention of the referee to any unsporting actions.

k. He authorizes substitutions if requested by team captains or coaches.

Linesmen

Position

a. In International matches atleast 4 linesmen should be appointed who should stand in free zone between 1m to 3m from each corner of the court, on the imaginary extension of line they control. From service corner, back lines should be controlled and from opposing corner, side lines should be controlled.

b. If instead of 4, only 2 linesmen have been appointed, they should stand diagonally opposite each other, one at each end of playing court at corner away from service zone.

Responsibilities during the Match

If only 2 linesman have been appointed, they should

sit at diagonally opposite corners of the court at a distance of 1 meter in indoor games while 3m in outdoor games. Each linesman has to keep a watch on side lines and end line nearest to him and to give signal to referee. They should raise their flag in while ball is out and drop in downward direction when ball is in.

When any player of receiving team gets touched by an Out Ball, Linesman can be requested by the referee to indicate this by giving signal from his flag.

Linesman will indicate to referee errors made by players while making the service or in a situation when ball goes out of vertical side markers completely.

Referee

Referee has full control over the game and every player is required to respect his decision. From beginning of play to end of match all players are considered to be under authority of Referee.

He is required to answer all the questions of players and can overrule decision of other officials when he is not satisfied by their judgment. In order to clear view of the game he should be positioned at a height of 50cm above one end of the net. Players, coaches and managers behaving in an unsportsmanlike manner can be penalised.

Location of First and Second Referee

a. For First Referee a stand at one end of net is made. He should be suited at a height of 50cm above the level of upper edge of the net.

b. Second Referee will stand in opposite site from where he can face the first referee. He should be along the extension of front zone of receiving team at moment of service.

Right of First Referee

a. He can give judgment on any matter relating to game;

b. He has the power to direct the whole match from beginning to end and issue directions to all officials in performing their duties.

c. He has to decide whether the playing court is in proper condition for play or not.

d. His decisions are final and are binding on all the players. He can overrule of any official if he is not satisfy with their judgment.

e. It is the responsibility of both first and second referee that ball to be used fulfils all specifications. No ball which does not fulfils specifications should be used.

Duties of the First Referee

First Referee will perform following duties during the match:

i. He will give signal and will penalise fouls committed by players;

ii. Only he can decide upon faults involving the server, the positions of the serving team, screening, the contact of the ball when in service trajectory, the faults in contacting the ball, the faults over the net and its horizontal bank, whether a simultaneous fault was committed or not and so forth.

iii. If captain is not agree with explanation of rules given by referee, at end of match first referee is required to give his authorisation to register this protest.

First Referee has to perform following duties before commencement of match:

i. He is required to control warm-up of team;

ii. He will perform toss up for service and court;

iii. Verify the condition of playing court as well as of all equipments to be used.

Duties of the Second Referee

On following occasions he should blow his whistle and give signal:

i. when ball touches the antenna on his side of court or crosses the net outside of crossing space;

ii. when any team committed positional foul;

iii. when under upper edge of the net a player touches either net or antenna;

iv. when back line player commits illegal attack-hit or blocking;

v. when any player get injured;

vi. when ball touches any outside object;

With help of Line-Up Sheet second referee will check the actual positions of players before beginning of each set.

Power of the Second Referee

Second Referee is considered to be the assistant of First Referee. He can replace First Referee if and only if because of any reason First Referee is not able to continue.

He has the right to perform the following:

a. Before and during all sets he verifies the position of players who are sitting on player's bench, and will make report to first referee about any misconduct of players;

b. Time-outs and substitutions made by a team are under his control and he will report First Referee and Coach about this during any interval;

c. He will supervise the conduct of all players and make a report to first referee for misconduct of any player;

d. He has the right to accept or reject request for interruption of game;

e. He make control on warming-up period of substitutes;

f. Whether surface of playing court should be dried up or not, should be decided by him;

Scorer

On opposite side of court to Referee and behind the umpire, Scorer should be positioned to perform the following duties:

a. He will record names and numbers of all players and substitutes on Score Sheet before beginning of each match.

b. He will record score, substitutions and number of time-outs requested during each set carefully.

c. He should announce number of time-outs requested during each set as soon as new request for a time-out has been made by any team;

d. He will verify that rotation order has not changed throughout the game;

e. He will record location of players on court before beginning of each set. On Score Sheet position of team serving first should be recorded first.

f. He will report to officials about number of requests made for time-outs;

g. After end of each set and after 8 point made by one of teams, he should announce the changing ends;

h. He should hand over the score sheet to referee and umpire for signature at end of match.

Location

Scorer's table should be positioned in opposite side from where he is facing the first referee.

Rights and Powers

a. During the game interruptions he can give signal to referee for errors in teams' line-ups or in team's service order;

b. He helps second-referee in doing registrations on score sheet, controlling legal interruptions and in making report to first referee, coaches and public.

Team Line-Ups, Location of Participants

Location of Substitutes and Coaches

a. On the bench which locates on the side of their

own court, substitutes and coaches should sit;

b. Those players whose name and number does not appear on Score Sheet should be considered substitutes for the set;

c. No player is allowed to talk to his teammate;

d. Outside the freezone of playing court, substitutes are allowed to take warm-up. This is only possible if they do not use a ball and return to their bench after taking warm-up.

Team Line-Ups

(i) The six players that begin a set compose the starting line-up of a team. The number of six players may not be reduced.

(ii) Before the start of a set each coach must present his starting line-up sheet to the scorer or the second referee.

(iii) The six players on the court make up the game line-up.

Tossing and Warming Up at the Net

Tossing

a. To decide which team will serve first and begin from which court, a toss should be made. This toss will be done by First Referee before entering in court. He will do so in presence of both team captains.

b. If both players score same points after completion of game and to decide winner a Deciding Set is to be played, again Toss should be made to decide sequence of play in this set also.

Teams Warming Up

a. A warm-up period of 3 minute will be provided to team before beginning of match if they previous had another playing court at their disposal, otherwise of 5 minute;

b. In case of consecutive warm-ups, team winning right to serve should take the first turn at the net;

c. Both teams will come near net for a period of 6 or 10 minutes if both captains request for warm-up simultaneously.

Beginning and Serving the Game

Service

Putting the ball into play is known as the Service. With his hand or any part of arm right-hand back line player will hit the ball over the net into his opponent's court. He will do it from service area.

As soon as ball is thrown by player in air, service is considered to have taken place. Server can hit the ball only once.

After striking the ball the player may land on the line or inside the court, so long as at the moment of impact he was behind the back line and within the service area.

Server is required to serve again if ball falls on ground after releasing from his hands without hitting. But, because of this no delay will be allowed in the game.

If after releasing from server's hand ball pass over the net without touching it, service should be considered to be good. Server should serve immediately after referee blow his whistle. Service done before referee's whistle

should be taken again.

Duration of Service:

Server will continue to serve till his team commits any foul.

USA Volleyball

Basic Principles for Service Order

Players are required to follow Service Order as stated in Line-Up Sheet

In following manner server will decide during the game:

a. Previous server will serve again if his team wins the rally;

b. Player of opponent team should serve if serving team commits any foul or its opponents wins the rally.

Conditions for Directing the Service

Before service First Referee should verify that:

a. Both teams are ready to play;

b. Player is who going to serve has possession of ball with him and he is standing in the Service Zone.

Following things should be kept in mind while making the service:

a. Within 5 seconds of First Referee's whistle service should be made;

b. Service should be done from service zone. Before touching the end line or free zone outside the service lines during service, he is allowed to move or jump freely. After hitting the ball, he can land within court or free zone.

c. After being thrown or released from hand but before touching the playing surface, ball should be hit with one hand or with any part of arm.

d. Service made before Referee's whistle should not

be taken into account and should be made again.

Serving In Second And Subsequent Sets

Right to serve get passed to both teams turn-by-turn, however, in deciding set server will be decided by making a toss.

Attempt to Serve

a. If after tossing server releases the ball from his hand, he is considered to have made attempt to serve, if ball did not touch the serve;

b. Referee should authorise to serve again after attempt to serve was made by the player. This service should be made by server within a period of 5 seconds.

c. No other attempt should be authorised.

Screen

At time of serving players of serving team are not allowed to wave their arms, jump or form groups to create problems for server.

Serving Faults

On following occasions referee will blow the whistle and signal the Change of Service:

i. when ball touches the net;

ii. ball passes under the net;

iii. ball touches any aerials or crosses net outside them;

iv. ball lands outside opponent's court;

v. before entering in opponent's court ball touches any player of serving side.

Serving Faults after hitting of Ball

In following conditions ball after being served properly becomes a fault:

a. To cross the vertical plane of the net it touches any object or any player of serving team;

b. Touches the net or an antenna or fails to pass through crossing space;

c. Passes above an individual or group screening;

d. Lands outside of the boundary lines of the opponent's court without having been touched first by an opponent.

Delaying in Game

Any act which delays the game should be penalised by Referee.

Serving Out Of Orders

Change of Service will be called by the Referee if any player makes the service when he is not entitled to serve. In this condition all points scored by the team during this period will be taken back. Players of faulty team will come to their correct position.

Rotation of Players

a. Players can change their positions at beginning of new set if new line-up has been received to scorer before starting of the set;

b. Before serving team to serve will rotate in a clockwise direction while changing the service;

c. In new set new rotation order can be used by the

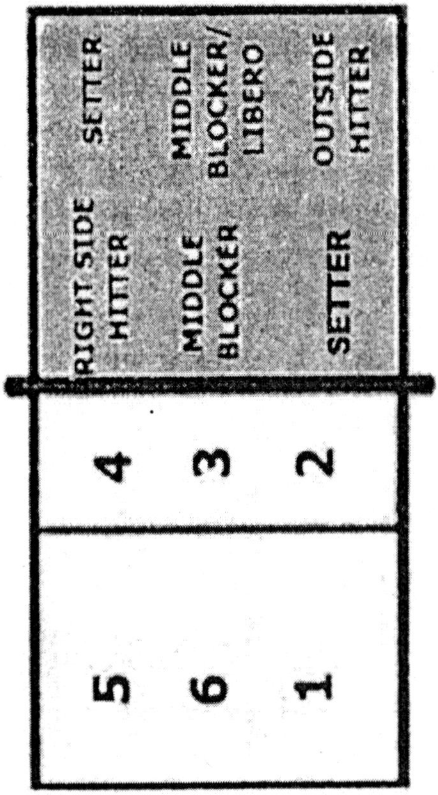

players and any player whose name and number has been recorded on score sheet can be registered in new starting line-up.

Rotational Fault

When service is made not according to service order,

Rotation Fault is considered to have committed. For this fault play can be suspended till correction of error and same penalty should be awarded to team as in case of Positional Fault.

Duration of The Game and Choice of Ends

Number of Sets in a Match

A match should consists of 5 sets.

Choice of Ends

To decide ends and order service, a toss will be made by captains of both teams.

Change of Ends

After each set both teams should change their ends, however, this rule does not apply in Deciding Set. Toss should be made again to decide order of service and ends in a Deciding Set.

Change of Ends In The Middle of the Deciding Set

Teams should change their ends if same number of sets has been scored by both teams and one team has scored 8 points in the Deciding Set. Previous server will again serve this time. If referee or captain of any team notices that they have forgotten to change their ends at proper time, they should do so as soon as mistake is get revealed by them.

Choice of End for Deciding Set

If both the teams scored same number of points during the play, a Deciding Set should be played for which toss should be made to decide ends and order of service.

Stoppage in Match

Following conditions should applied if play interrupts because of any reason:

i. If game is re-started on same court after one or more periods, but not more than 4 hours, the score in the interrupted set should not be changed, and game should be played again when will remain the same, and the game begins where it left off.

ii. If match is played again on another court, score of interrupted set should be annulled, but results of completed sets should not change. Cancelled set should iii. Whole match should be played again if delay exceeds more than 4 hours.

Allowable Interruptions

2 time outs and 6 substitutions per set is permitted.

Successive Requests for Interruption

The same team is not allowed to request two consecutive game interruptions for substitution unless the game has been resumed. But 2 or more players may be substituted at the same time.

Authorisation and Duration of Interruptions

a. Play can be interrupted for substitution only for time in which substituted player can go out of court and substitute enter into the court;

b. Only game captain or coach can request to stop the play for substitution;

c. Team which request time-out can reduce its time limit and has to re-star the game immediately;

d. Time-out should be of 30 seconds;

Interruptions of Play, Times-Out

i. No player is allowed to go out of court in time-out and to talk to anybody. During this period, players can get advice from their coach, but coach should not enter into court;

ii. Referee should grant time-out only when ball is dead or out of court. When captain or coach request to stop the match, he should specify clearly the reason of such stoppage, i.e., for substitution or for time-out. If nothing has been specified by him, referee will consider it a stoppage for time-out.

iii. If any captain or coach makes request for time-out for third time, he should be warned. If in same set offence is repeated again, team has to loose the service or opponents will be awarded the point.

iv. 2 time-outs of 30 seconds per set are permissible.

A team can request 2 time-outs consecutively without re-starting the play. After request for substitution, time-out can take place and after a time-out, substitution can take place.

Improper Requests

Referee should not accept the requests made in following conditions:

a. If a non-authorised team member makes the request;

b. Request made during a rally at or after whistle for service has been blown. If Second Referee blows the whistle for second time by mistake;

c. If before resumption of play same team request substitution for second time;

d. If any team request substitution when allowable number has been already exhausted, warning should be given to this team.

Interruption Faults

In following conditions team is considered to have committed the faults:

a. when after being called to resume the game it prolongs it time-out for second time;

b. when it requests a time-out for second time;

c. when after having charged with two consecutive time-outs, it is not ready to start the set. In this condition this team should be declare to be in default.

d. when after using 2 time-outs it makes a delay in substituting the players.

Interruptions Because of Team Members

a. Play should be stopped if any player gets seriously injured while playing;

b. To substitute a player who has been expelled, play should be interrupted.

i. If a player is injured and cannot continue to play, he must be legally substituted.

ii. If no substitution is possible the first referee gives 3 minutes to the injured player.

iii. If the legal substitution is not possible, the first referee shall authorise an exceptionally illegal substitution for the injured player.

iv. If the injured player does not recover within 3 minutes the team is declared incomplete.

Duties and Responsibilities of First Coach should be performed by Assistant Coach if First Coach has been expelled from the play.

Prolonged Interruptions During a Match

If play has to be stopped because of any unexpected reason, First Referee, Organisers and Jury should decide the manner by which normal conditions will maintain. For this following procedure should follow:

i. If game has to be stopped for more than 4 hours, whole play should be played again.

ii. if match is re-started on same playing court, game should be started with same set at which game was interrupted with same score, players and game position. Points scored in previous sets should not be changed.

ii. if match is re-started on another playing court, set in which such interruption was caused should be cancelled and played again with same starting line-ups and game positions. Sets which have been completed will keep same scores.

Change of Courts

a. Before beginning of each set teams should change their ends, whereas substitute players and other team members have to change their benches.

b. Team should change their courts as soon as one of scores 8 points, however no player should get any kind of instruction from referee and players should not change their positions. Player serving before change will serve again this time.

If teams have forgotten to change courts at proper time, they should do it as soon as they come to known the fact. Score should not be changed after change of court.

Interval Between Sets and Changes of Courts

Between sets an interval of not more than 2 minutes is allowed, whose duration increases to 5 minutes between fourth and fifth sets. The teams must line-up on their end lines at the moment they are called by the first referee to resume the match.

Substitutions

i. Play can be stopped for not more than 3 minutes if an injured player is to substitute, and this period should not be considered as a time-out. This stoppage should be allowed only if it is not possible to replace the injured

player. Referee will stop the play as soon as any player get injured.

ii. Play should be started again immediately after injured player has substituted and no player is allowed to get any kind of advice from coach.

Change of Service

When serving team commits any foul, service should be changed.

Side-Out

With call out of Side-Out, service order should change.

Play at the Net

a. Ball should be thrown in such a way that it crosses the net completely within two vertical side markers and lands in opponent's court.

b. If inspite of landing into opponent's court, ball touches any player, no foul should be charged again server.

c. Play should not be stopped if ball touches net between vertical side markers in course of play.

Double Fault is committed if two opponents touch the net at the same time.

d. Ball which hits the net between vertical side markers should be played again if player does not touch the net.

Ball Touching the Net

Ball Crossing the Net

a. Space in the vertical plane of the net is called Crossing Space. This space is limited by upper edge of the net and on the sides by antennas and their imaginary extensions.

b. Ball should be thrown in such a way that it crosses the vertical plane of net within crossing space.

Ball Touching the Net

While passing through the crossing space, ball can touch the net.

Faults Committed during crossing up of ball over vertical plane of net

In following conditions a team sending the ball into opponent's court commits a foul of Ball Out:

a. If ball crosses the vertical plane under the net completely;

b. If ball contacts with any person or object which is outside from boundaries of court, ceiling or part of net.

i. If ball goes out of vertical plane outside the crossing space;

Ball in the Net

a. Play should be cancelled if ball rips the mesh of net or brings the net down.

b. If ball has not touched the floor, ball driven into net can be recovered.

Hitting the Ball

a. A player can use any part of his body to hit the ball.

b. Three attempts to throw the ball are provided to each team. In third attempt ball should cross the net and land on opponent's court.

c. Held Ball: Ball is considered to be held if any player is having it in his hands or arms. Scooping, lifting, pushing or carry of ball is also considered as Holding of Ball.

d. Ball can be touched with any part of the body of player.

e. Contact with Ball: Player who touches the ball is considered to have played the ball.

f. Double Hit: A player who hits the ball for more than one time with any part of his body is considered to have commit Double Hit.

Contact with Ball

Ball in Play

From the moment service is delivered by server till referee blows his whistle, ball should be considered to be in play.

Allowable Number of Contacts

Three attempts should be provided to each team to throw the ball into his opponent's court.

a. No player other than blocker can touch the ball more than once.

b. If any player touches the ball, he is considered to have contacted with the ball.

Simultaneous Contacts

Two or more players can contact the ball simultaneously.

a. If two opponents contact simultaneously over the net and ball remains in play, receiving team should provided the right to get third contact;

b. If two teammates contact at the same time, team should be considered to have two contacts.

Team on opposite side of net should be considered to have committed the foul if ball falls to the ground outside

of playing court.

Characteristics of the Contact

a. Ball can be contacted with any part of player's body.

b. If contacts are done simultaneously, hit is correct and bounce is clear, ball can contact various parts of the body. However, during the first contact of a team if the ball is not played overhand with fingers, it may contact consecutively various parts of the body.

c. Ball should be hit clearly and be in moving position. In any direction it can be rebound.

d. Movements of players after or before contact with ball should not be taken into consideration by the referee while judging the contact with ball.

Faults in Ball Contact

a. A player is liable to commit Double Contact foul if he contacts the ball more than once in succession;

b. Player commits a Head Ball fault if he does not clearly contact the ball or lets it come to a momentary rest;

c. Players will commit Double Fault if two opponents are holding the ball at the same time over the net;

d. Player who contacts with ball with any part of body under the waist, commits Illegal Contact fault.

e. If a team contacts the ball more than thrice, it commits a Four Contacts fault.

Physical Contact

i. In order to contact the ball a player can push his teammate;

ii. A player can hold his teammate who is likely to make commit a foul;

Hands Passing over the Net

After the Smash: Passing hands over the net after a smash is permitted.

During The Block: Touching the ball with the hands over the net in the opponent's court before the opponent's attack is completed is a fault.

Simultaneous Touch

Ball played by two players of the same team:

If two or more players of the same team attempt to play the ball and the ball is touched by only one of them, this shall be considered as one touch only.

A player may play the ball while in contact with a player of his team. However, no player may be used as a means of support to reach the ball. It is permitted to hold back a player who is about to commit a fault.

When two players of the same team contact the ball simultaneously, it is considered as two hits.

Simultaneous touch by opposing players:

When opposing players hit the ball simultaneously above the net, the player of the team opposite to that receiving the ball is considered to have touched it last.

After such a simultaneous hit by opponents, the team whose side the ball enters has the right to play the ball three times. If after the simultaneous hit the ball lands on the playing area, the team on whose court it lands is penalized; if the ball lands outside the court, however, the team on the opposite side of the net is at fault.

If the ball is held simultaneously by two opposing players, it is a double fault and the point is played again.

When the ball, having touched the top of the net as well as the opponent's block, returns to the attacker's side, the players of this side have the right to three hits.

Double Fault: When two opponents commit a fault simultaneously, it is a "double fault" and the point is played again.

Block

Blocking: (a) Any player taking part in a blocking action in the course of which the ball is contacted, shall have the right to make a second play at the ball. Such a second shot, however, shall count as the second of the three hits allowed to the team.

(b) The three back-line players may not block at the net but may play the ball in any other position near or away from the block.

(c) The blocking action is made near the net and consists of attempting to stop the ball coming from the opposite side with any part of the player's body above the waist.

The block can be performed by any or all of the front-line players. Any player is considered as having the intention to block if he places one or both hands above the level of the top of the net while in a position close to the net.

A block is a blocking action in which the ball is contacted by one or more of the players concerned.

(d) The hands of the blockers may reach over the net, but the blockers shall not contact the ball over the opponent's court until after the completion of the opponent's attack.

(e) If the ball touches one or more players in the block it will be counted as only one hit for the team, even if these contacts are not made simultaneously by the players in the block.

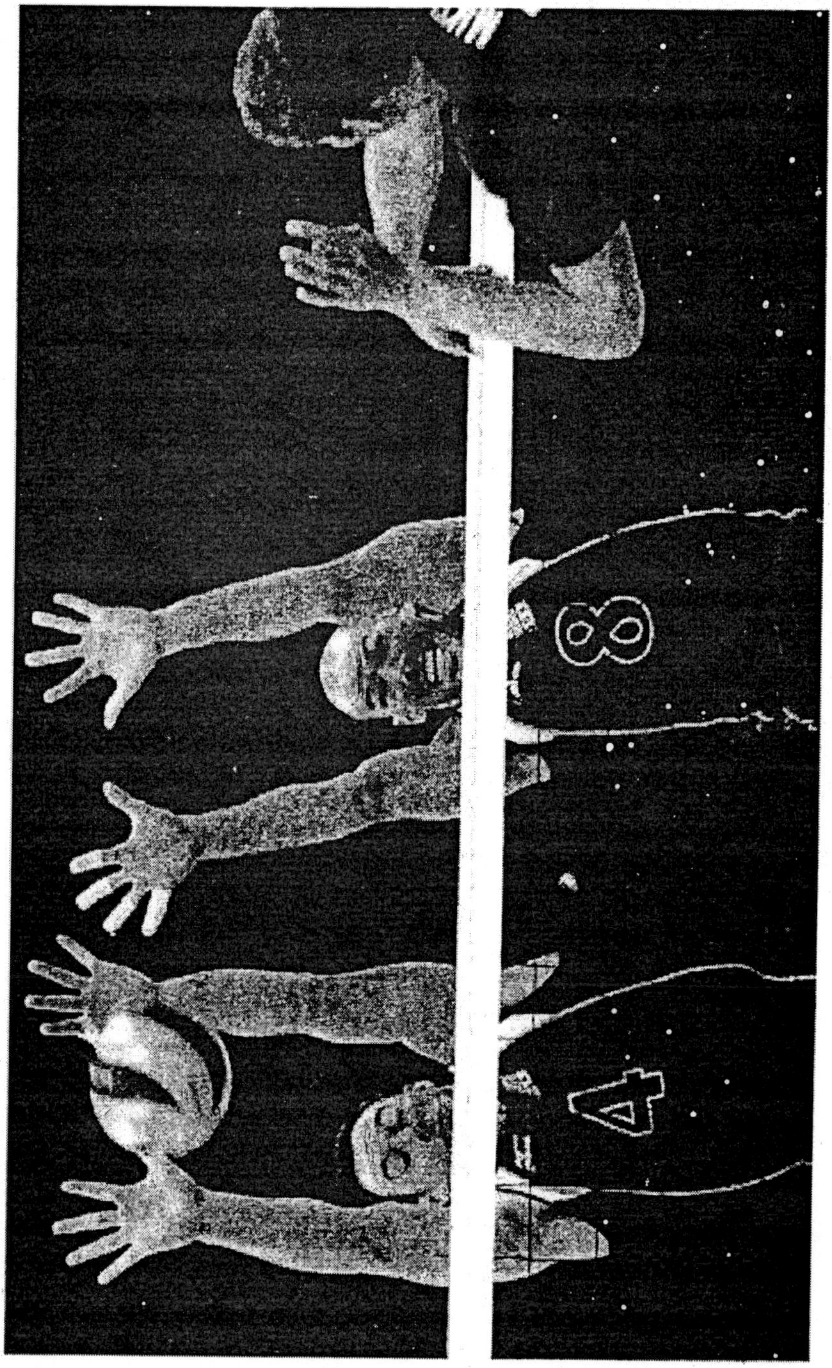

Blocking Contact

(i) In blocking, the ball may be contacted with the hands or arms and touch the head or another part of the body above the waist of the blockers.

(ii) Consecutive contacts may occur by one more blockers, provided the contacts are made during one action.

Contact Subsequent to the Block

(i) The first contact after the block may be made by any player, even if he had touched the ball during the block.

(ii) Block does not count as a contact.

After blocking, a team is entitled to 3 more contacts to send the ball to the opponent's court.

(iii) If a player makes an attempt to block separately and a distance from an individual or collective block and touches the ball blocked before, he makes the first team contact.

Blocking within the Opponent's Space

(i) The block is permitted if the ball is blocked after the opponent has executed an attack-hit.

(ii) One or more blocker may make an attempt to block or block by passing their hands and arms over the net, as long as this action does not interfere with the play of an opponent.

Blocking Faults

A blocker commits a fault when:

(i) He interferes with the play of an opponent in the opponent's space, either before or during the action.

(ii) He blocks outside the antennas and touches the ball in the opponent's space.

(iii) He blocks the opponent's service.

(iv) As a back line player he is effective or participating in a block.

Back-Line Players

(i) Back-line players may not take part in a block.

(ii) Back line players may not direct a ball from within the attack area into the opponent's court unless the ball is below the height of the net.

From behind the attack line they may, in any way permissible, hit the ball into the opponent's court.

A back-line player smashing from the back court may land on or in front of the attack line, provided his take off for the smash was clearly behind the attack line.

(iii) As the attack line extends indefinitely, a back-line player may not hit a ball into the opponent's court from above the height of the net if he finds himself to be outside the court, but within such extended limits of the attack area.

Crossing the Centre Line

(i) Crossing the vertical plane of the net:

Crossing the vertical plane of the net with any part of the body with the purpose of interfering with or distracting an opponent while the ball is in play is a fault.

Crossing the vertical plane of the net without touching an opponent or the opponent's court is not a fault.

(ii) Contact with the opponent's court:

Contact of any part of a player's body with the opponent's court during play constitutes a fault.

Touching the opponent's court with one's foot is not a fault provided that some part of this foot still remains in contact with the centre line.

It is not a fault to enter the opponent's court after the referee has whistled to stop play.

Decision and Protests

(i) Any dispute concerning an interpretation of the

rules must be resolved on the spot by the referees. Only the captains of the disputing team may speak to the referee.

(ii) The decision of the referee cannot be appealed during the match.

(iii) Protests: If the explanation of the referee, following a protest of the captain, is not satisfactory, the captain may appeal to a higher authority. The referee shall continue to control the game and will later make out a report concerning the protest.

Ball Out of Play

(i) Ball landing outside: The ball is considered to be out when it touches the ground or any object outside the playing area.

A ball touching any line is in.

(ii) Ball touching the net outside vertical side markers: A ball touching the net outside the vertical side markers constitutes a fault.

(iii) Dead Ball: The referee's whistle stops all play. The ball is then dead.

Scoring and Results of the Game

(i) A set is won when a team has scored 15 points and has at least a two point lead over their opponents.

If the score is tied at 14/14, the set continues until one team has a lead of 2 points.

(ii) It is a fault when a team fails to return the ball over the net correctly. This fault will be penalised by the opposition winning a point or service.

(iii) Forfeits: The game shall be forfeited by a team which refuses to play after the referee has asked for the game to be started. The score will be recorded as 15/0 for each set, and three sets to nil for the match.

This does not apply when the game is uncompleted

due to injury.

Team that scores a point

Only the team that serves scores a point, if it wins the rally either because of its playing actions or because the opponent commits a fault called by the referee.

Winner of a Match

(i) The winner of a match is the team that wins 3 sets.

(ii) If a team becomes incomplete for the rest of the match, the opposing team will be given the points and the sets it needs to win the match.

(iii) A team that for no justifiable reason does not appear on the playing court in due time is in default and his opponent is given the same scores, 15-0 per set and 3.0 for the match.

(iv) If, after receiving a warning from the first referee, a team refuses to play it is declared in default and the opponent is given by default the score of 15-0 for each set and 3.0 for the match.

Penetration into the Opponent's Space and Court

Each team must play within its own court and related playing space, except in the following cases.

Contact with the Net

(i) Once he has hit the ball, a player may touch the poles, ropes or any other object outside of the 9.50 m length of the net, if it does not influence the play.

(ii) It is forbidden to contact the net, all along its length including the antennas.

(iii) When a ball is driven into the net and causes the net to contact an opposing player, no fault is committed.

Hands crossing the vertical plane of the net

(i) After the attack-hit, it is permitted to across the hand over the net if the contact was made in the player's own playing space.

(ii) During the block, it is permitted to contact the ball above the net within the opponent's space, provided that the player does not interfere before or during the opponent's play.

(iii) A ball in play that is heading towards the opponent's court, through the external space or the space below the net, may be returned by a teammate provided it has not yet completely crossed the vertical plane of the net or its imaginary extension when such contact is made.

Contact with the Opponent's Court

(i) To touch the opponent's court with a foot or feet is allowed, provided that some part of the encroaching foot or feet remains in contact with or above the centre line.

(ii) With the exception of the feet, it is forbidden for a player to contact any part of his body beyond the centre line within the opponent's court, while in play.

(iii) A player may enter into the opponent's court after the referee has whistled to finish the rally.

(iv) A player may contact the free zone surrounding the opponent's court, as he does not bother or interfere with an opponent in play.

Penetration Faults

A penetration fault is committed when a player:

(i) Interferes with any other ball contact in the opponent's space.

(ii) Touches a ball in the opponent's space before or during the opponent's attack-hit.

(iii) Penetrates into the opponent's space, from the beneath the net and touches, bothers or interferes with an opponent.

Faults and Sanctions

When participants commit faults during the game due to actions contrary to the rule or due to misconduct, the first referee judges the fault and determines the sanction applicable, in accordance with the following principles:

Consequences of a Fault

(i) Depending upon the case a penalty means that the opponent to the team committing the fault gains a point or the right to serve.

(ii) There is always a penalty to a fault.

(iii) If two opponent's commit a fault simultaneously the penalties cancel each other and a play-over is called.

Game Faults

These are individual actions or team movements contrary to the rules of the game and they consist of:

Not sending the ball correctly over the net into the opponent's court.

Misconduct

Behaviour towards officials, opponents, spectators or teammates may be incorrect, and depending upon the degree of the offence, conduct must be sanctioned as:

(i) Rude Conduct. If the participant acts contrary to good manners, moral principles or his action is the expression of contempt toward the referee, opponents or spectators.

(ii) Unsportsmanlike Conduct. If a participant delays the game, coaches the team when it is forbidden to do so, shouts, intimidates the opponents or argues with the players, referees or spectators.

(iii) Aggression. If a real, physical attack or an initiated aggression against a referee, an opponent or the spectator is made.

(iv) Offensive Conduct. If any aggressive attempt at personal honour is made by means of insulting words and gestures to a referee, opponents or a spectator.

Sanctions Scale

(i) The repetition of a misconduct by the same member of the team during the same set calls for the gradual application of sanctions, according to the misconduct sanction scale.

(ii) Disqualification due to aggression does not call for any previous sanction.

Sanctions for Misconduct

Depending on the degree of the incorrect conduct according to the judgement of the first referee, the sanctions to be applied are:

(i) Penalty, for rude behaviour. It must be registered on the score sheet and the opposing team will gain a point or the service.

(ii) Warning, for unsportsmanlike conduct. No penalty is given but it warns the players or teams from a second unsportsmanlike conduct for the remainder of the set.

(iii) Expulsion and Disqualification. Offensive conduct is sanctioned by expulsion and it means that the player is not allowed to play for the remainder of the set. Aggression is sanctioned by disqualification, and it means that the player must leave the playing area for the remainder of the match.

OFFICIAL VOLLEYBALL SIGNALS

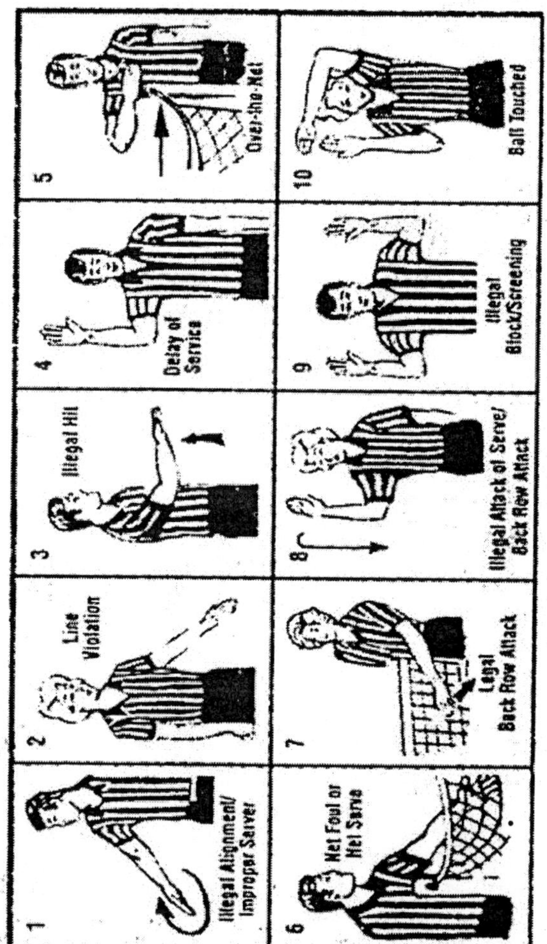

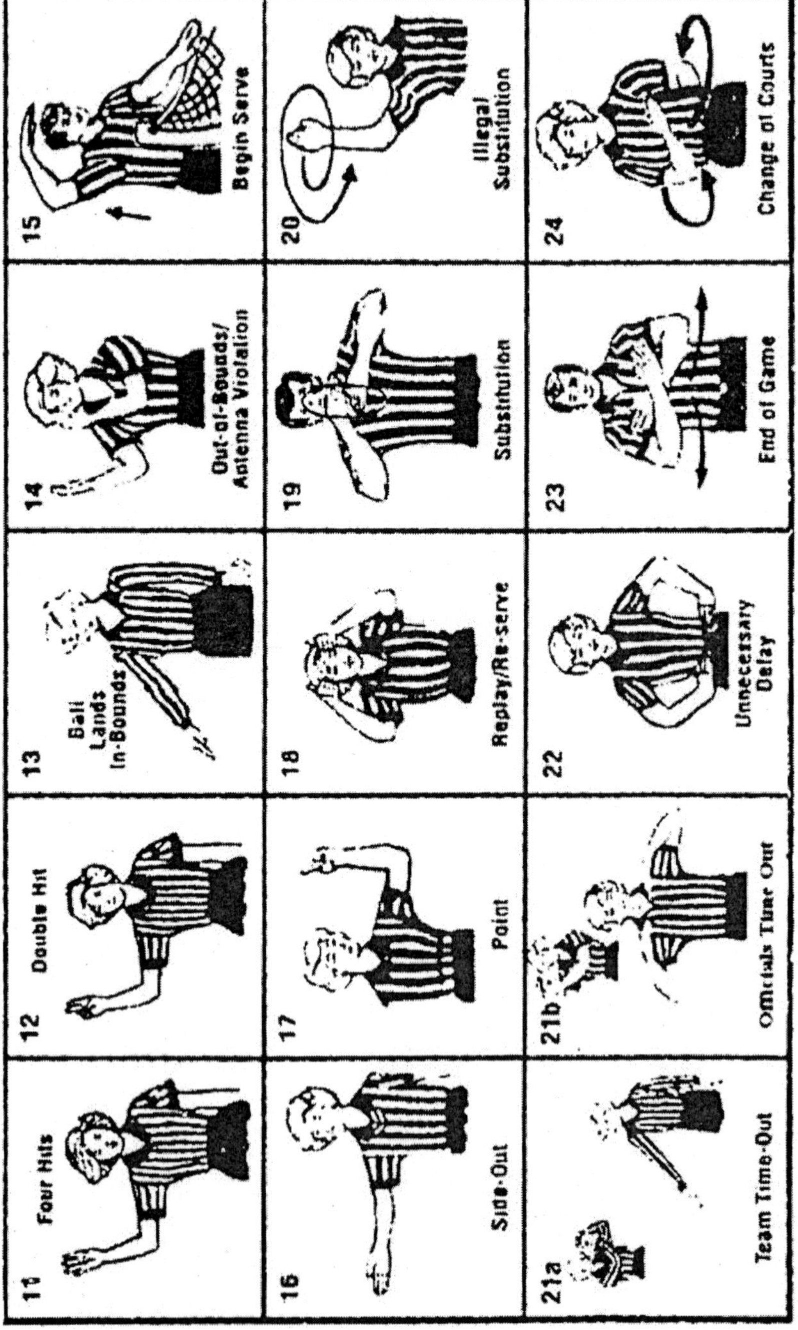
11 Four Hits
12 Double Hit
13 Ball Lands In-Bounds
14 Out-of-Bounds/Antenna Violation
15 Begin Serve
16 Side-Out
17 Point
18 Replay/Re-serve
19 Substitution
20 Illegal Substitution
21a Team Time-Out
21b Officials Time Out
22 Unnecessary Delay
23 End of Game
24 Change of Courts

LINE JUDGE SIGNALS (using flags)

Basic Volleyball Official Responsibilities

First, the host team/school (or tournament site director if you're at a tournament) has the final ruling in all matters.

Volleyball referees are next down on the ladder. The referee must follow all the guidelines and ground rules set by the site/tournament host. The referee follows all other matters concerning the rules of volleyball.

The Referee is in Charge of the Match

The referee is in charge of the match and what the referee says goes.

If you are a volleyball referee, from the moment you arrive on site you are in charge of the court. Your authority extends over other officials, coaches, and players.

If any issues arise you need to take charge. For instance, if the scorekeeper would make a mistake in the score, you need to help correct the mistake if you can.

The work crew (scorekeeper, assistant scorer, second referee, line judges, etc) are there to assist you. As the first referee, you have the authority to over rule or if needed, replace a member of the officiating crew.

If a situation were to arise where crowd behavior was affecting play, the host management needs to take care of the situation. This is usually done by a volleyball official alerting the site/school administrator of the problem.

Samc with issucs with coachcs or playcrs that cscalate

to the point where coaches or players need to be removed from the court.

Basic Volleyball Referee Responsibilities for Game Situations

The referee controls the flow of the match

How the referee Interacts with players, coaches, and other officials impacts how the match is run. How you blow the whistle and timing is important. Signaling is communication. Blowing the whistle, signaling, verbally communicating with players/coaches, etc... all these things factor in to how well the match runs.

The Serve

Before you whistle and beckon for serve, scan the court. Look at all the players, coaches, and officials to make sure everyone is ready to play.

Before the serve is the time for teams to do line up checks, substitutions, or timeouts because these things must occur during dead ball situations. So be ready and anticipate these situations. The better you are able to anticipate, the less problems you will have.

Referee Hand Signals

The First Referee is in charge of calling ball handling. Obviously, it's important to follow the ball and watch for illegal contacts (doubles, lifts, etc). The Second referee can make signals to you for ball handling, but it's the First Referee's responsibility to make the call.

How you decide to communicate with the Second Referee should be discussed before the start of the match. For instance, the First Referee may prefer the

Second Referee communicate during play using various hand signals.

For instance, for some signals the Second Referee may discreetly signal to the First referee during the play. These discreet signals include double contacts, four hits, back row attacks, back row blocks, and the ball contacting the ground.

Second Referee Responsibilities

The Second Referee is mainly in charge of communicating with each team's coach and the other officials at the scorers table. The main calls made by the Second Referee are players crossing the centerline and players touching the net during play.

The Second Referee is also in charge of whistling timeouts and substitutions.

Calling Timeouts and Substitutions

If a team is wanting to sub or call a timeout (during a dead ball situation) the First Referee should signal "timeout" to the Second Referee. The Second Referee then takes charge of the court by whistling the timeout/ sub. At the end of the timeout/sub, the Second Referee whistles and signals indicating the court is being given back to the First Referee. The First Referee is now again in charge to administer the serve.

Using Cards

The First Referee can administer cards to players or coaches to get control of situations.

It's important to think of cards as "the last line of defense".

A good volleyball official will hardly ever need to issue cards because good officials hardly ever have situations escalate that far out of hand.

BASIC PROCEDURES FOR CONDUCTING A USA VOLLEYBALL MATCH/COMPETITION

FOR REFEREES

These are the basic procedures to be followed when conducting official USA Volleyball matches or competitions. More detailed information for each of these items can be found in the USAV Referee Guidelines and Instructions.

1. OFFICIALS

a. The officials should be certified USA Volleyball referees and scorers.

b. The prescribed USA Volleyball uniform and certification patch should be worn by all officials.

c. At a minimum, referee equipment includes a whistle with lanyard, a set of yellow/red cards, a flipping coin and a watch or timing device.

2. ARRIVAL

a. Officials should arrive at the playing venue no less than 30 minutes prior to the start of the competition and should locate the tournament director or event manager.

b. Determine playing formats, ground rules, warm-up procedures and any other protocols.

3. MATCH PREPARATION

a. Referees should examine the court and playing

equipment prior to the first match: identify court lines, any floor obstructions and playing area; determine rulings for overhead obstructions; examine the playing equipment (including net, posts, referee stand and game balls); verify the net height and ball pressure.

b. Scorers should ensure pens, pencils, score sheets and Libero tracking sheets are available at the scorer's table. Lineup sheets and rosters may also be required.

4. OFFICIAL'S PRE-MATCH DUTIES

a. Prior to the coin toss, the first and second referee should discuss their match responsibilities, as well as communication techniques that will be used between them during the match. This should include: discreet help from the second referee; addressing conduct issues; and ensuring consistent application of ground rules.

b. Preferably prior to the coin toss, or immediately thereafter, the referees will meet with the officiating crew to give instructions to the line judges (first referee) and scoring crew (first or second referee).

c. Conduct a coin toss between the team captains prior to the start of the timed warm-up period. During the coin toss, the first referee may designate one team as "heads" and the other team as "tails."

Once tossed, the coin should be caught and the result immediately revealed.

d. After the coin toss, the first referee will supervise warm-up periods and may request the second referee to time their duration.

Note: In the event a team does not choose to use its time on the court, the court shall remain unoccupied.

e. During the warm-up period, the first referee should verify the legality of each team's player and Libero uniforms. All players must wear uniforms.

f. At the end of the warm-up period, the first or second referee will blow a whistle to indicate that the warm-up period is over and players are to clear the court.

g. Referees and other officials take their assigned places.

4. START OF THE FIRST SET OF THE MATCH

a. Teams line up on the end line of their respective team court. When both teams are ready, the first referee will blow a whistle and motion for teams to take their positions on their court.

b. The second referee, using each team's lineup sheet, and the scorer will verify that players are in the correct positions as listed on the official lineup sheets submitted by each team. No corrections may be made unless an error or omission has been made by the scorer prior to the start of play.

c. Upon completing the lineup check, the second referee should permit any Libero replacements to occur and confirm that the assistant scorer has recorded them.

d. The second referee then delivers the game ball to the first server of the match. The whistle is blown and a visual sign is given by the first referee for service to begin. This marks the time the set officially begins.

e. Prior to the serve, serving team players should halt their movements to allow officials to determine their positions. Continual or distracting movement may be construed as screening. The first referee must be aware of screening during each serve of the match.

5. DURING THE MATCH

a. Each referee has specific duties and responsibilities during the match as outlined in Rules 23 and 24. The USA Volleyball Referee Guidelines and Instructions helps clarify these responsibilities.

b. Judgment and ball handling decisions, as well as match control, flow and tempo, are very important for any first referee.

c. Match administration (substitutions, timeouts, etc), communication with the team benches and scorer's table, and positioning/focus during net play are important aspects of working as a second referee.

d. Line judge, scorer and assistant scorer duties are clarified in Rules prescribed by FIVB, respectively. Additional information can be found in the USA Volleyball Referee Guidelines and Instructions.

6. PROCEDURES FOR REGULAR GAME INTERRUPTIONS

a. Substitutes should approach the substitution zone and wait to be recognized for entry. For multiple substitutions by the same team during a dead ball period, each player and his/her substitute must enter the substitution zone in succession, one pair at a time and must wait until entry is authorized by the second referee. For multiple substitutions by the same team, there can be no delay between incoming substitutes. When opponents request substitutions simultaneously, the second referee must ask that one team wait while the other substitution is administered and recorded.

b. When the coach or playing captain requests a timeout, the second (or first) referee should immediately whistle, show Signal 14, Timeout, and then indicate the team by pointing, open-handed, toward that team's bench. After 30 seconds have elapsed, the second referee must blow a whistle to end the timeout. Teams should immediately retake the court. Both referees display the number of timeouts each team has taken, and then the first referee prepares for the next rally.

7. END OF THE SET AND START OF THE NEXT SET

a. A set officially ends when the whistle is blown for the fault resulting in the winning point. The set interval begins when the first referee executes Signal 13, End of Game. Following the whistle indicating the end of a set, the referee will direct the teams to change playing areas and benches immediately, with the exception of the deciding set. The players proceed to their right until they reach their new bench area with the team on the left passing the first referee and proceeding directly to the bench.

b. Two minutes and 30 seconds after the interval begins, the second referee will blow a whistle and teams shall immediately report to the court and line up in their proper positions to start the set.

c. When a deciding set will be necessary, the teams follow a different procedure at the end of the set prior to the deciding set. The first referee will release the teams to their respective benches. The captains for each team then immediately meet at the scorer's table, where the first (or second) referee will conduct the coin toss for the deciding set. Once the choice of sides has been determined, thefirst referee whistles and directs the teams to their appropriate team areas, using the procedure specified in 7a above if a change of court is necessary. Procedure for the start of the deciding set is the same as stated in 7b.

8. CHANGE OF TEAM AREAS DURING A DECIDING SET

a. When teams are required to change team areas during a deciding set of a match, the first referee will blow a whistle and show Signal 28, Change of Courts. Teams will change playing areas without delay with player positions remaining the same.

b. Substitutes and other team personnel will change team areas.

c. If requested, the second referee will verify that players are in their correct positions on the court.

9. AT THE END OF THE MATCH

a. Following the whistle indicating the last rally of a match, the first referee will whistle again and display Signal 13, End of Match, and direct the players of each team to line up on the end line of their team court.

b. When both teams are in position, the first referee will blow a final whistle and motion for the teams to proceed to the center of the court to shake hands with the opponents.

c. The second referee will ensure that the game ball

is returned to the designated area for safekeeping.

d. Both team captains shall thank the referees.

e. The first referee will then review the score sheet to verify the final results. Signing the score sheet by the first referee is optional.

e. Referees will then immediately depart the playing area.

5

VOLLEYBALL TERMINOLOGY

A

Ace

A serve that hits the floor in bounds, is shanked or cannot be handled by the receiving team, immediately resulting in a point for the serving team.

Antenna

Fiberglass or plastic rod secured to the net on both sides as an extension of the sideline. The ball must cross the net inside the two antennas.

Approach

Footwork used to run and jump to attack the ball.

Assist

A set or bump set that leads to a successful attack.

Attack

A ball hit by a jumping hitter in the front or back row which attempts the ball across the net and into the opponent's court.

Attack Line

The line on the volleyball court that separates the front court from the back court, located three meters from the net on either side.

B

Backcourt

The area of the court behind the three meter line

Back Set

A set to the right side hitter, usually positioned behind the setter

Back Row Attack

An attack from behind the three meter line. Also the name of a rule violation in which a back row hitter attacks from in front of the three meter line

Biq

A back row quick set, meaning a low fast set to a backrow hitter, usually just over a quick middle attack

Block

An attempt to stop an opponent's attack by putting up two straight arms in front of him/her

Block Attempt

Jumping to block a hitter but not being able to touch the attack

Block Assist

A stat that goes to the blocker who jumped next to the blocker who blocks a ball for a point

Bump

The act of passing a volleyball with the forearms

C

Center Line

The line in the middle of the volleyball court directly under the net

Closing the Block

When the middle blocker travels to get directly next to the outside blocker leaving no space in between the two.

Cross-Court Shot

Hitting the ball to the opposite side of the court

Cut Shot

An off speed cross-court shot with spin

D

Decoy

When a hitter jumps for a quick set in an attempt to draw blockers away from another hitter.

Dig

Preventing an attack from hitting the floor by passing it so that it is retrievable by a teammate.

Dink

A soft attack off of the fingertips, also known as a tip.

Dive

When a player leaves his/her feet to contact or dig a ball.

Double Block

When two blockers attempt to stop and attack.

Double Hit

An illegal contact in which the ball touches a player twice in succession.

Double Quick

A play in which two hitters approach for a quick set.

Down Ball

When an attacker hits the ball overhand while standing on the ground, usually off the net. When the offense recognizes that the ball will be hit in this manner, they back off the net and do not block.

Dump

When the setter pushes the second ball over the net

instead of setting it to a hitter.

E

Error

When a contact is unretrievable by a teammate or results in a point for the other team. A shank is a passing error, a hit into the net is an attack error.

F

Facial

When the ball hits a player in the face.

First Referee (Up ref)

The referee on the stand responsible for starting and ending plays and ultimately has the last word on points and sideouts.

Five-One (5-1)

An offense in which there are five hitters and one setter. The setter sets all the time, whether in the front row or the back row.

Five Set

A high back set behind the setter to a hitter on the right side of the court.

Floater

a type of serve that does not spin and moves unpredictably in a floating fashion.

Foot Fault

When a server steps on or over the line in the process

of a serve.

Forearm Pass

A skill in volleyball in which the ball is propelled by the forearms.

Four Hits

A rule violation in which a team contacts the ball four times in one possession. Only three contacts are allowed.

Four Set

A high set to the left side hitter.

Four-Two (4-2)

An offense in which there are two setters and four hitters. The player in the front row acts as setter giving the team two hitters in the front row in any given rotation.

Free Ball

When a team cannot get an attack and instead sends the ball over the net with a forearm pass.

G

Game

A series of plays and rallies between two teams that continues until one team reaches the pre-determined number of points (15, 21, 25 or 30.) To win, a team needs to win two out of three games or three out of five games. After 2008, the word set is used instead of game.

H

Held Ball

A violation in which the ball stops moving during the

contact. Usually called on a set.

Hit

An attack or spike usually utilized on a team's third contact. A player approaches, jumps, and swings striking the ball downward and across the net to the other team.

Hitting Percentage

A stat determined by calculating the number of attempts divided by the number of kills

Hole

A space between blockers in the act of blocking.

I

In

When a ball hits the floor inside the lines of the court or when any part of the ball touches the line.

J

Jump Serve

A type of serve in which a player uses an approach and leaves the ground for contact.

Joust

When two blockers reach a ball on the net at the same time, trapping it between them and each try to make the ball fall on the opponent's side. Usually won by the player to apply the latest pressure.

Jungle Ball

When volleyball is played by inexperienced players

K

Kill

An attack that is put on the floor on your opponent's court or is not able to be retrieved, resulting in a point

Kong Block

A one-handed block

L

Left Side Hitter

A front row player's position also known as the outside hitter, hits and blocks mostly on the left side of the court.

Libero

A defensive specialist position added to the game in 2001. This player wears a different shirt than his/her teammates and plays only in the back row.

Lift

A violation in which the ball is pushed in such a way that it stops its motion during a forearm pass or a set Line

The boundaries of the court including the sidelines and end lines. Blocking line means to take away the attack down the closest sideline. Hitting line refers to hitting the ball along the nearest sideline. Only applies to attacks occurring at or near antenna.

Line Shot

When a hitter on the left or right side hits the ball along the nearest sideline instead of across the court toward the opposite sideline.

Linesman

An official responsible for calling the ball in or out and block touches.

Let Serve

When a serve hits the top of the net but still makes it over to the opponent's side. Before 2001, this was a service error, but now it is to be played by the receiving team.

M

Middle Blocker

A position in which the player is expected to block all hitters no matter what their location and who hits mostly in the middle of the court. This player will often hit quick sets.

Mintonette

The original game of volleyball when it was invented in 1895 based on badminton, basketball and tennis.

N

Net

The item at center court that separates the two teams. The women's net is set to a height of 7'4" and the men's net is set to a height of 8'0".

O

Off-speed Hit

A change up in which the attacker does not hit the

ball full strength but instead sends a slow spinning ball usually to an open position on the court.

One Set

A low, quick set to the middle just in front of the setter.

Open-hand Tip

A soft shot attack in which the hitter uses his fingertips to place the ball on the court.

Opposite

The player positioned three spots away from the setter (or opposite the setter). This player usually hits on the right side.

Out

When the ball falls completely outside the lines of the court or hits the antenna placed on the net.

Outside Hitter

The player who hits and blocks on the left side of the court.

Over

A violation in which a blocker reaches over the net and interferes with the path of the ball when it is completely on the opponent's side of the court.

Overhand Pass

When a receiver passes the ball with her hands over her head.

Overhand Serve

A serve in which the player tosses the ball with one

hand and strikes in the air above her head.

Overlap

A violation in positioning of the players on the court.

P

Pancake

A dig in which the player gets the ball up by placing a flat hand on the ground (palm down) and letting the ball bounce off the back of his hand.

Pass

A skill which allows a player to transport the ball to another place by using his forearms or hands. Also see overhand pass and underhand pass.

Penetration

When a blocker reaches over the net in order to block the opponent's attack. It is legal to reach over to block a ball as long as the ball is traveling across the net.

Pepper

A warm up game with two players facing each other. Player one tosses the ball to player two, player two underhand passes the ball back to player one. Player one sets the ball to player two, player two hits the ball to player one, Player one digs the ball to player two and the rally continues until one of the players makes a mistake.

Perimeter Defense

A defense which entails the line digger staying deep on the line, the middle back slides to the hitter's side and the right back remains in position to dig the angle.

Pipe

A backrow set to the middle of the court for a back row attacker.

Player Replacement

Act of the Libero either coming into or leaving the game.

Playing Captain

The player on the court who represents his/her team and is the only team member who can talk to the referee.

Points to Win

15 or 25 points is required to win a set; in order to win, a team must be at least 2 points ahead (Competition management may determine other limits in certain situations).

R

Rally

The act of playing the ball back and forth over the net

Rally Scoring

Each play results in a point unless a replay is directed

Red Card

A sanction resulting in the ejection of a player/coach from the set for rude or unacceptable behavior with no point being awarded

Replay

When an official instructs the team to play over the

previous point due to an error or other reasons

S

Serve

The technique of putting the ball into play

Setter

A player (usually the second team contact) who delivers the ball to a hitter

Side Out/Rotate

When the team wins the serve from the opposing team, the team will rotate one position clockwise, often referred to as a Side Out

Spike

A hard driven ball into the opponent's court, usually accomplished by hitting the ball with an overhead arm swing.

Substitution

The act by which a player enters a set to occupy the position of another player who must leave the set.

T

Time-Out

A suspension of play requested by the playing captain or coach and granted by the R1; the length of the time-out is governed by rule

Touch

A ball that is touched by a player either intentionally

or accidentally; both count as a touch

Y

Yellow Card

A warning to a player/coach for unacceptable behavior that results in a point for the other team

W

Wipe

When the attacker deliberately hits the ball so that it bounces off the blocker's hand and goes out of bounds.

6

WARM-UP DRILLS FOR VOLLEYBAL PLAYERS

Loosen up in the warm-up

The warm-up is a critically important part of volleyball practice. It allows the players a chance to get their muscles ready for the impending workout while giving them an opportunity to ease back into the skills they'll be developing throughout the practice session. A typical warm-up consists of a light jog, a full-body stretching session, and a series of volleyball warm-up drills.

Remember, these volleyball warm-up drills shouldn't be too intense. They are not designed for athletic conditioning or muscle strengthening. Rather, they have been developed to reawaken everyone's muscle memory and get them accustomed to the basics of the game like serving, setting, and bumping.

Pass the Pepper!

Pepper is one of the most useful volleyball warm-up drills since it covers a variety of skills in a fast-paced manner. This variation of Pepper involves 4 players. To begin, divide the team into groups of 4. For this drill, player 1 is the hitter, player 2 is the setter, and players 3 and 4 are diggers, and they stand in a circle facing each other.

At the start of the drill, player 1 has the ball. They toss it up in the air, and hit it towards one of the two diggers. The digger pops the ball back up towards the setter, who sets it back to the hitter, who hits it towards one of the diggers. Play continues in this manner until the coach blows the whistle, signaling a change in positions.

If one of the players misses the ball and it falls to the ground, each member of the Pepper team must drop and do 10 push-ups or run to the nearest line and back 3 times. This will lead players to become more accurate with their hits, sets and digs, and prevents laziness when reaching for the more difficult shots.

Serves and Bumps

A good serve can make or break a volleyball game. Since serving is one of those key skills in volleyball, it's important to include a volleyball serving drills or two in the volleyball warm-up drills. This serving drills focuses on developing accuracy.

To begin, have the players stand in a line at the serving area. The player at the front of the line starts a bucket of balls. The purpose of the drill is to serve the ball into each of the 6 areas on the opposite side of the court. Area 1 is the back right of the court, area 2 is the front right, area 3 is the front center, area 4 is the front left, area 5 is the back left, and area 6 is the back central area of the court.

While serving, the player keeps track of how many serves it takes for them to complete the circuit and serve to all 6 areas on the court. If running this drill as a mini-competition, the player with the lowest score at the end of the drill is the winner.

Finally, here's a simple drills that focuses on bumping called the "Two-Line Bump". Divide the team into 2 groups, and have each group stand in a line facing the other group approximately 10 feet apart.

The player at the start of the line has the ball, and they bump it to the player facing them on the other line. That player bumps it to the next person on the line across from them, and so on. If the ball falls or is bumped to the wrong player, play starts over from the beginning of the line.

DRILLS FOR VOLLEYBALL PRACTICE

Shoulder Warm Up Drills For Volleyball Practice

All teams should have drills for volleyball practice for shoulder warm up. A good shoulder warm up can help prevent shoulder problems from developing.

Volleyball players need shoulder exercises for improve shoulder flexibility, mobility and stability.

Overhead Broomstick Dislocations

Purpose

The purpose of this exercise is to improve the mobility around the shoulders.

The Movement

Hold a broomstick, rope, or towel in front of your hips with a wide overhand grip. Slowly move the bar up overhead and back behind your body. You should feel a stretch in your chest and shoulders.

Continue back to the start position following the same path. Make sure not to bend at the elbows or arch your lower back too significantly.

Activating the Serratus Anterior - Drills For Volleyball Practice

Scap Push Up (Push Up Plus)

A scap push up is basically a push up without any movement at the shoulder or elbow joints.

Purpose

The main purpose of scap push ups is to strengthen and activate the serratus anterior muscle. When shoulder dysfunction is present, often the first muscle to stop functioning properly is the serratus anterior. Training the serratus anterior helps prevent shoulder dysfunction by holding the scapulae tighter to the ribcage.

The Movement

Start in push up position. While keeping your arms straight, lower your body towards the floor bringing your shoulder blades together.

If you aren't strong enough to do this from the floor position, you can do this exercise standing with your hands against the wall.

Strengthening External Rotation - Drills For Volleyball Practice

External Rotation

A volleyball players external rotators of their hitting shoulder are predominantly weaker than their non hitting shoulder.

Purpose:

Strength rotator cuff muscles with shoulder external rotation.

The Movement:

From a standing position, externally rotate the shoulder using an elastic band.

This exercise can also be done lying on the side using a light weight.

Scapular Stability - Drills For Volleyball Practice

Standing Y

Purpose:

Strengthen the muscles that stabilize the scapula.

The Movement:

Bend over at the waist to a 45 degree angle. Straighten your arms at the elbows and hang them down in front of you with your thumbs pointed out.

Quickly raise your arms up with your thumbs pointed up during the movement forming a Y with your arms.

Standing T

Purpose:

Strengthen the muscles that stabilize the scapula.

The Movement:

Same starting position as the Standing Y.

Quickly raise your arms up with your thumbs pointed up during the movement forming a T with your arms.

Standing W

Purpose:

Strengthen the muscles that stabilize the scapula.

The Movement:

Same starting position as the Standing Y except bend elbows to 90 degrees, put arms in front of your chest, and point thumbs up.

Pull your arms back as you bring your shoulder blades together.

Dynamic Shoulder Flexibility - Drills For Volleyball Practice

PNF Diagonals

Dynamically stretching the shoulder muscles.

Purpose:

Improve movements at the shoulder.

The Movement:

Bring the arms across the body, following the same path of movement with each repetition. As you move the arms across the body, switch the direction of the thumbs. On the higher hand, point the thumb up. On the lower hand, point the thumb down.

Remember this exercise should be dynamic. Gradually increase speed based on your stretch tolerance.

These are just a few exercises for shoulder warm up drills for volleyball practice.

There are many more exercises that can be done at practice such as medicine ball push ups, over head shoulder shrugs, band face pulls, band internal rotation, band pulls, side planks, and wall stick ups.

■ ■ ■